# CELEBRATING BLACKPOOL

JANET RIGBY

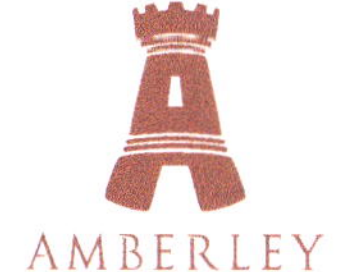

AMBERLEY

First published 2023

Amberley Publishing, The Hill, Stroud
Gloucestershire GL5 4EP

www.amberley-books.com



British Library Cataloguing in Publication Data.
A catalogue record for this book is available from the British Library.

ISBN 978 1 3981 0414 3 (print)
ISBN 978 1 3981 0415 0 (ebook)

Typesetting by SJmagic DESIGN SERVICES, India.
Printed in Great Britain.

# Contents

# Introduction

Blackpool, like most towns and cities, has had much to celebrate. Celebrating brings to mind events such as victory celebrations, jubilees or local events like the opening of a theatre, leisure facility or iconic building. Blackpool is unique in that most of its attractions are exclusive to the resort. As far back as 1885, a journalist said about the opening of the new tramway: 'Nothing in the nature of a public improvement has been allowed to come into existence without a befitting inaugural ceremony.'

From the opening of the first branch railway in 1846 to the inauguration of a new promenade and drinking fountain, reported in the *Illustrated London News* (1870), all were celebrated in style. At the opening of the Winter Gardens in 1878, Alderman Cocker generously footed the bill for the civic heads of sixty-eight cities and boroughs in England, plus the Lord Mayor of London, to attend a banquet and grand ball, and to be his guests at the exclusive Imperial Hotel. It is not recorded what this bill came to, but it must have been huge; nevertheless, Dr Cocker settled the account unflinchingly. Blackpool has never been afraid to advertise itself widely. From the beginning of the First World War until 1940 it had its own Inquiry Bureau in London, which advised on rooms along with railway and bus services, as well as employing staff to extol the virtues of the resort. The office windowsill had a large model of the Promenade illuminated at night.

A leading example of Victorian enterprise that is famous throughout the world, Blackpool Tower is a Grade I listed building, officially designated as being of outstanding architectural or historic interest. Blackpool can also boast of having five buildings and other edifices listed as Grade II*, which includes particularly significant buildings of more than local interest. The thirty-three Grade II listed buildings of special architectural or historic interest include five situated on the Pleasure Beach – the White Tower Casino and four of its historic rides. There are also around sixty blue plaques commemorating the places of historic interest where people lived or worked, and one green plaque on the Grade II* Grand Theatre commemorating the famous theatre's architect, Frank Matcham – considered by many to be his masterpiece.

The first electric streetlamps were switched on in Blackpool, later becoming the world-famous Illuminations. The opening of the first electric tramway in 1885 resulted in three centuries of trams, and the town is the only one in England to have operated a tramway to the present day.

The resort had the good fortune to have been home to men of stature like Alderman Cocker, followed by the Bickerstaffe brothers, Messrs Bean and Outhwaite and the Thompson family, whose contribution to the amazing success story of Blackpool is legendary. Another Blackpool family can now be added to the list: the Sedgwicks, a family of fourth-generation showmen who invested heavily into the town, now owning all three piers and several other amusement venues.

At the beginning of 2020, the *Blackpool Gazette* marked the start of the decade with the words 'a decade of change and excitement awaits with the resort to be completely different by 2030'. Whatever happens we must never lose sight of Blackpool's humble origins, from a small hamlet to the thriving entertainment centre it is today.

# People of Enterprise and Endeavour

## Founding Fathers of Blackpool

On 18 April 1911, crowds gathered to pay their final respects to a man who was described in his obituary as 'the maker of modern Blackpool' and about whom was said 'no person living today so embodies the spirit of Blackpool'. William Henry Cocker had an unbroken record of over forty years serving the local authority, and his entrepreneurial spirit was instrumental in the development of the town as the country's leading holiday resort.

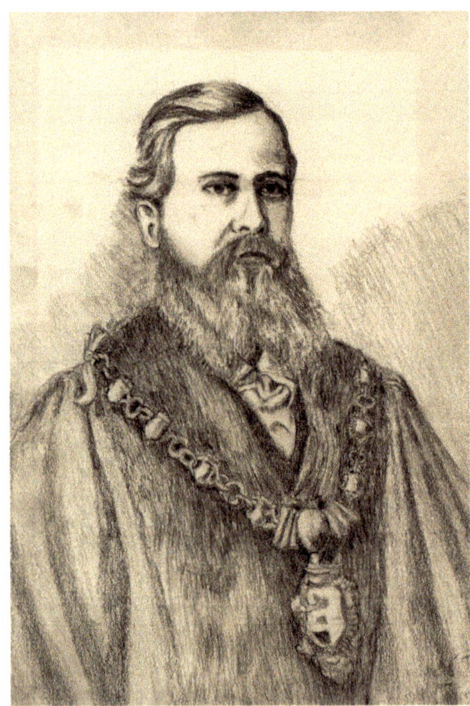

Alderman Cocker, pictured here in his mayoral robes.

William was born into a prominent landowning family on 9 December 1836 in Hygiene Terrace, which was situated on the Promenade. His father, John, a doctor, had conveniently married into the family of Henry Banks, who owned a vast estate in Blackpool and in 1851 had purchased the mansion Bank Hey and built the first assembly rooms in the town. His son, William, who was a qualified surgeon like his father, made a surprising career change when in 1873 he gave up his medical practice to establish Dr Cocker's Aquarium, Aviary and Menagerie, which later became part of Blackpool Tower. Visitors flocked to see the magnificent exhibits on display. Dr Cocker served as the first mayor when Blackpool was granted its charter of incorporation as a borough in 1876, serving a three-year term.

On the day of his funeral a procession left his home and travelled to St John's Parish Church. This impressive spectacle included a firing party of the local Territorial Artillery and the Blackpool Lifeboat Band. A total of thirty carriages, one of which was carrying many floral tributes, were followed by six horses drawing a gun carriage bearing the coffin draped with a Union Jack. The remaining carriages took immediate relatives, the mayor, town clerk, ex-mayors, aldermen, councillors and other public officials.

Dr Cocker was well known throughout his civic career for his lavish entertaining, and it is little wonder that he ended up in relative poverty in a modest house in Whitegate Drive. Yet, five years after his death in 1916, the *Blackpool Gazette* reported that despite his contribution to the town, Dr Cocker lay in an unmarked grave. His lasting memorial, however, is a clock tower in Stanley Park, dedicated to him in 1926.

## From Seafarers to Entrepreneurs

Of all the local families associated with the progress of Blackpool, one stands out as a success story of gigantic proportions. From humble beginnings as local fishermen taking visitors out to sea in a small rowing boat, the Bickerstaffe family were described as 'appearing to have been indigenous to the soil of Blackpool and to have been born and bred between wind and water'.

Pleasure steamers operated in Blackpool for over a hundred years, from the mid-1840s to the mid-twentieth century, and were made popular by the opening of the first pier (now North Pier) and the South Jetty (now Central Pier) in 1868. Boats were launched on the seafront running excursions to North Wales, Barrow-in-Furness, and Peel on the Isle of Man. Robert Bickerstaffe Sr (1807–79) continued to expand his business by building the Wellington and Pier Hotel, near the South Jetty (owned by the Bickerstaffes), which became the starting point for steam trips. The first major vessel to ply her trade was the *Bickerstaffe*, built in 1879 at Laird's shipyard in Birkenhead, which on its maiden voyage back to Blackpool carried a large party of invited guests, including the mayor, Dr Cocker,

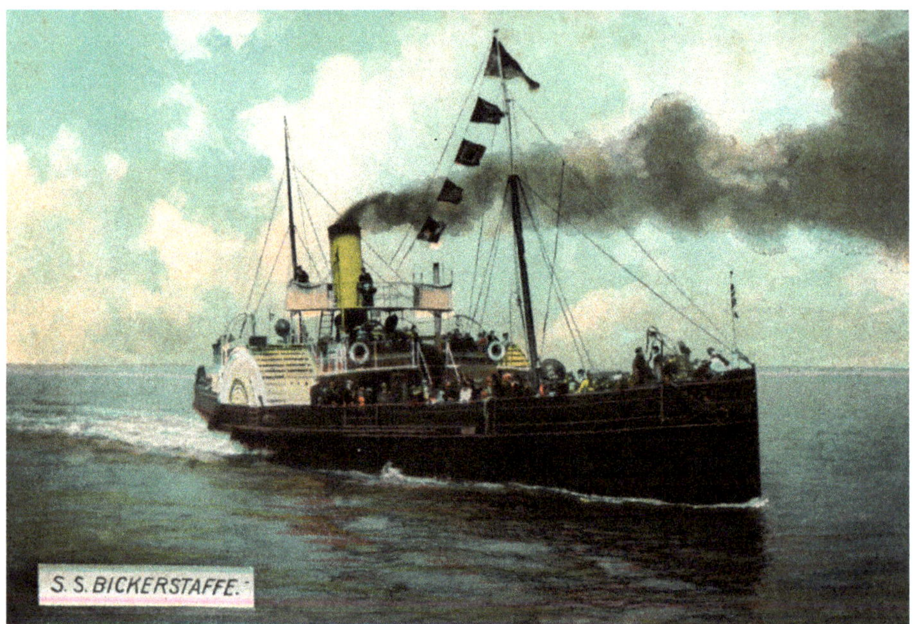



SS *Bickerstaffe*.

and members of Blackpool Council, including Robert and John Bickerstaffe. As the vessel reached the landing stage on the South Jetty after a journey of one and a half hours, thousands of people were awaiting its arrival.

Robert Bickerstaffe Jr, often referred to as 'Cousin Bob' was the nephew of Robert Sr and cousin of John Bickerstaffe, who continued the business of his uncle, helping to develop the Wellington Hotel site and the pleasure boat business. In 1870, Robert became pier manager and introduced cheap steamer trips to Southport. The trippers, upon their return, were welcomed back with a band, which encouraged them to remain on the pier and spend their money there.

Robert was the coxswain of Blackpool's first lifeboat, the *Robert William*, launched on 14 January 1864. Over 20,000 people watched as the new lifeboat was towed, in a boat carriage pulled by four horses, from the lifeboat station to the seashore. He was nominated for the silver medal of the Royal National Lifeboat Institute for his bravery and skill – and that of his crew – during the rescue of four people from the schooner *Bessie Jones* of Fleetwood, which was wrecked during a heavy north-west gale on Salthouse Bank on 26 February 1880. Having served as coxswain for two terms, from 1864 to 1869 and 1876 to 1887, Robert Bickerstaffe was awarded a medal on his retirement in 1887.

The Bickerstaffe brothers helped to establish the famous Blackpool Lifeboat Band by starting a subscription list. Thanks to the generosity of fifteen prominent citizens, the band –the only one of its kind in the world – raised large sums of

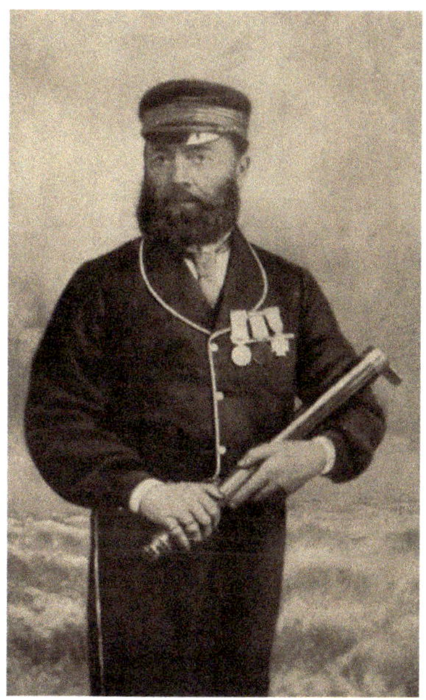

*Right*: Robert Bickerstaffe, coxswain.

*Below*: Wellington and Pier Hotel.

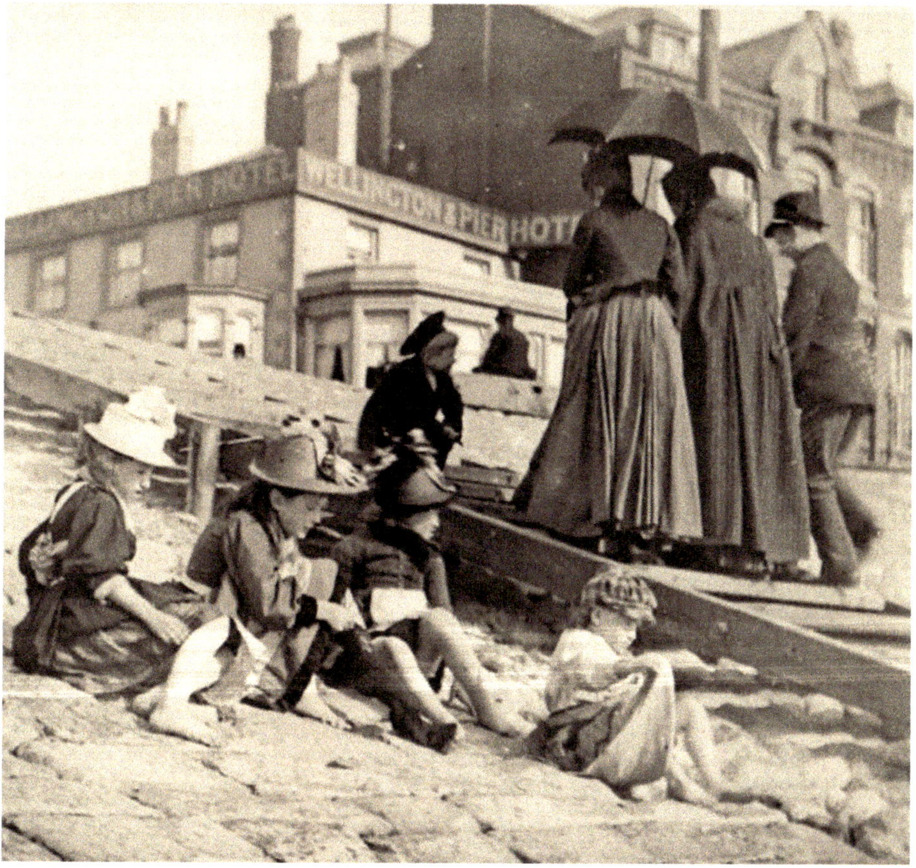

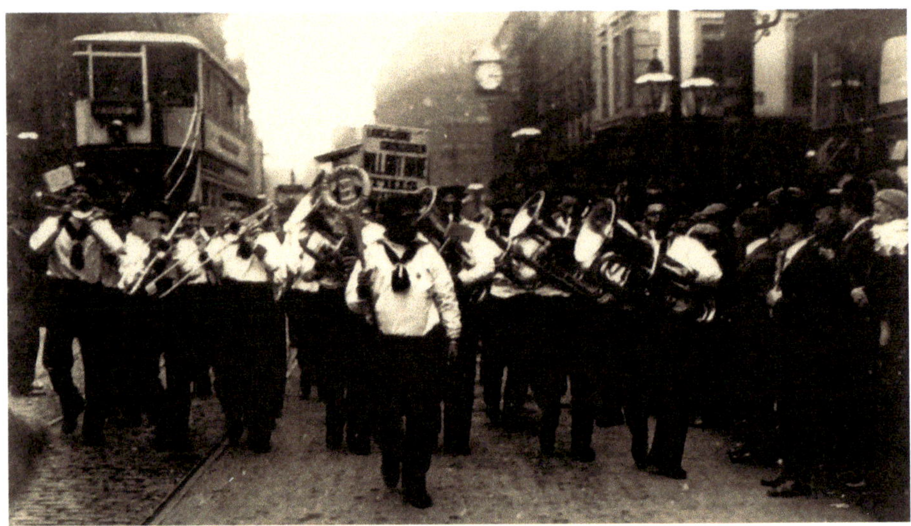



money for charitable causes. In 1935, they celebrated their golden jubilee as guests of Mayor Alderman G. Whittaker and his councillors. In 1940, the Lifeboat Band finally put down their instruments and this unique band was no more.

John Bickerstaffe, dubbed 'Father of Blackpool Town Council' and 'Mr Blackpool', started his working life as a boatman, also serving as a member of the crew of Blackpool's first lifeboat under his cousin Robert. A shrewd businessman, he held many roles in the town, serving as mayor from 1889 to 1891, and sitting on several committees. He also held directorships of the South Jetty Company and Electric Tramway Company, as well as being proprietor of the Wellington and Victoria hotels and a major shareholder of the Winter Gardens and Palace Gardens. His activities in the town increased still further when he became founder and president of Blackpool Football Club and the Blackpool and Fylde Victuallers Association. However, John Bickerstaffe was soon to embark on his most ambitious project for the town: the building of the famous Tower, for which he would become universally famous and receive a knighthood for.

John Bickerstaffe's younger brother, Thomas (1860–1934), also took an active role in civic life. He was said to have 'helped to build up one of the great pleasure centres of the world, and in his spare time advertised Blackpool to the four corners of the earth'. He served as mayor from 1925 to 1926 and when the jubilee celebrating the town's incorporation as a borough was held, tribute was paid to his 'versatility and energy'. For over thirty years Thomas was chairman of the resort's Publicity Committee and the Winter Gardens Pavilion Company, and director of C&S Brewery. When his brother died in 1930, he took over as chairman of the Tower Company. He died in 1934 at the age of seventy-two.

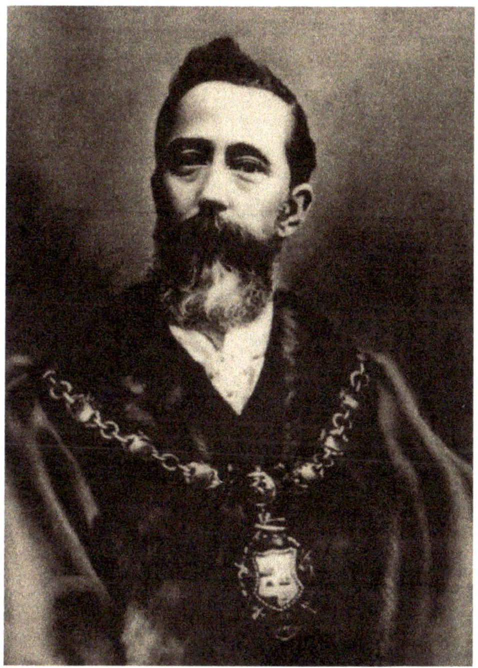

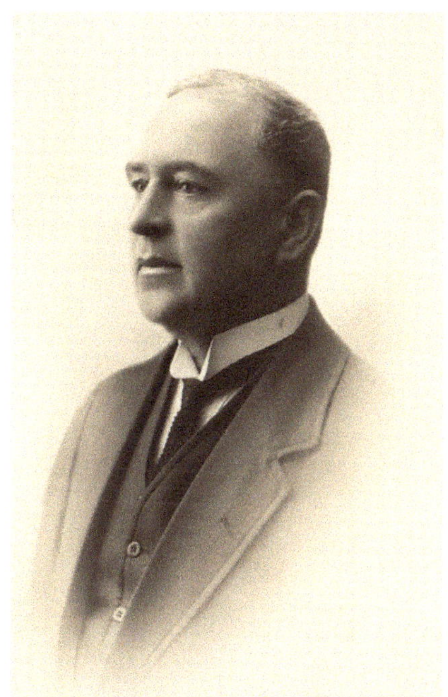

*Above left*: Mayor John Bickerstaffe, *c*. 1890.

*Above right*: Thomas Bickerstaffe.

## End of a Dynasty

The Bickerstaffes' long association with Blackpool came to an end with the death of Tom's son Douglas in 1964. He had continued to run his father's steamers until the decline of the industry in the 1930s, joining the Tower Company Board in 1937 and becoming its chairman in 1947. He remained on the board until 1961 when the ownership of the Tower passed to EMI.

## John Charles Robinson, the Man Who Designed Blackpool

Blackpool Council was fortunate in having a gifted borough architect. John Charles Robinson, from 1920 to 1944, was responsible for designing many features of the Promenade, including the open-air baths at South Shore, the lift tower on the cliffs, colonnades, and shelters. He also designed the café on Stanley Park, Derby Baths, the technical college, the municipal offices, St John's Market, Talbot Road bus station, the Collegiate School for Girls, and the crematorium chapel. He was known for paying particular attention to decorative details and

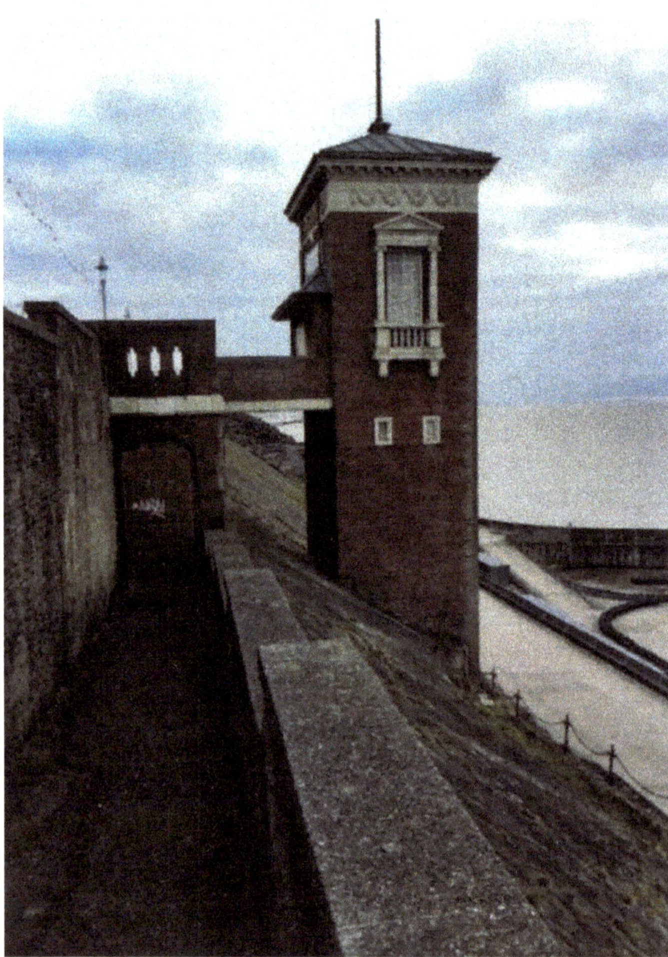

Cabin lift on
Queen's Promenade.

good quality fittings, and when the budget did not stretch to this it was not unknown for him to pay out of his own pocket.

In 1938, he was involved in the town's most ambitious civic scheme yet, which meant the removal of Central station to Chapel Street and the demolition of the terraced housing on the Bonny estate, to be replaced by a new civic centre, including a boulevard with fountains, a new town hall, shops, and a theatre. With the start of the Second World War these plans were put on hold and never revived, and the proposed site is now home to Coral Island and car parks. John Charles Robinson's modernistic designs, many of which still survive, include the Grade II listed Cabin Lift on Queen's Promenade, which was built in 1930 in the Classical Revival style to transport visitors from the top of the cliffs to the lower promenade. A front portion of the building, which once housed a waiting room, was demolished some time ago. The lift was closed in 1979 due to cliff subsidence but is still an interesting feature of the North Promenade.

# Celebrating the Growth of Blackpool

'Progress of Blackpool' was the local newspaper headline in June 1877, when it reported on the festivities to celebrate the completion of works recently carried out to provide new attractions for the increasing number of visitors. The year 1876 had been a busy one for Blackpool, celebrating its incorporation as a borough and the election of its first mayor, William Henry Cocker. A new promenade, an extension to North Pier, and an Indian Pavilion had all added to the town's prosperity. Another exciting project was nearing completion: an enormous building of glass and iron with a 3,000-seat concert room, costing £100 – the illustrious Winter Gardens.

Crowds were entertained with firework displays, Promenade concerts and music by the band of the 94th Regiment, followed by an evening torchlight procession along the Promenade and main streets. The Indian Pavilion on the

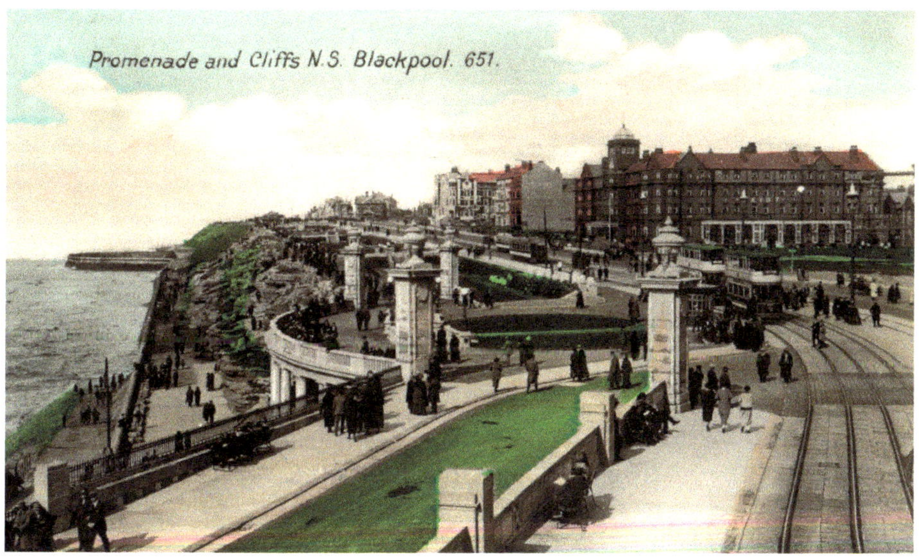


Promenade and cliffs, North Shore.

new pier hosted a grand banquet, presided over by the Mayor of Blackpool. Most of the public areas were decorated with bunting, and a decorative triumphal arch had been erected. Flags flew from many of the windows in Talbot Square, where the drinking fountain was festooned with brightly coloured Venetian masks.

The opening of the two piers in the 1860s marked the steady progress of Blackpool attracting more visitors. The new promenade, commencing at South Shore and extending northwards until joining the Claremont estate, just north of the Metropole Hotel, had opened to the public in April 1870. It had cost £60,000 and it was said at the time: 'It now forms one of the finest and noblest promenades in the country.' The Promenade became an important feature of early holiday resorts, providing a platform for the visitors to take in the sea air, to admire the view, and to see and be seen. More importantly, it allowed everyone to 'promenade', regardless of their social status. Hundreds of flags decorated the streets leading to the Promenade, where the triumphal arch stood at the corner of Talbot Square, inscribed with the words 'The Gate of Health' and flanked by the figures of a lifeboatman and volunteer fireman bearing the mottos 'Always Ready' and 'Always Willing'.

The procession was headed by the Volunteer Corps, members of the Masonic Lodge, and invited guests in nine carriages: engineers and contractors, friendly and trade societies, and local schools. The local trades were represented by carpenters and joiners planing and door making, blacksmiths shoeing a horse, and butchers on horseback, including one riding a donkey. At the centre of the triumphal arch

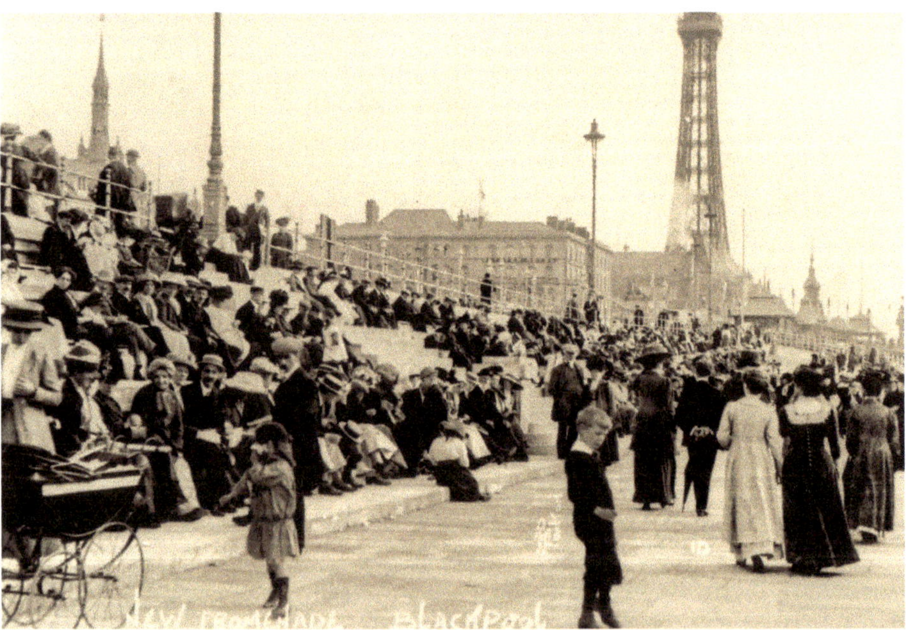

New Promenade, Blackpool.

near the Clifton Hotel stood the figure of Britannia holding a trident. An onlooker remarked that Britannia kept moving about in the most ungainly manner, nodding its head to the crowds below and frequently taking off its golden helmet for some air, providing much amusement for the audience.

During the Easter holidays of 1905 and in June of that year, the *Leeds Mercury* reported: 'Blackpool is the most wonderful place for amusements, and it is not likely that these will suffer now that the visitors will be able to get from pier to pier without walking on one another's heads.'

A reception was held at the Palace Ballroom that was attended by over a hundred mayors and mayoresses from all over England. A fine spectacle of 200 carriages carrying over 1,000 guests accompanied the mayor and corporation along the Promenade. Escorted by three bands, the procession passed along the carriage drive to the northerly end of Queens Drive at the Gynn public house, proceeding to the southerly end of the Promenade before returning to a point between the Tower and the Palace buildings. A total of 5,000 children from the local schools, all dressed in their Sunday best with faces scrubbed clean, waited for the procession holding commemorative handkerchiefs adorned with pictures of the seafront, the Blackpool coat of arms, and portraits of the mayor and borough surveyor. The guests then alighted from their carriages, the mayor declaring the works open. The previous evening a mayoral banquet had been held at the Hotel Metropole.

A trip was also arranged for the guests of the corporation to travel by train to Fleetwood for a cruise around the coast on the Royal Mail Steamer *Duke of Connaught* and thousands watched motor speed trials along the Promenade, which had been organised by the Blackpool and Fylde Motor Club.

The year 2009 saw the completion by Blackpool Council of an award-winning project scheme to rebuild the entire 3.3-km length of the Promenade, which would create five new headlands and sea defences. The Tower Festival Headland, built out onto the beach, is a large outdoor events space in front of the Tower, with pebble-shaped seats and ten lounger seats cast into the concrete pavement to resemble giant pebbles washed up on the beach. The Blackpool World Fireworks Championships are staged there each September during the illuminations season, lighting up the Promenade and the sky. The Great Promenade Show represents an outdoor art gallery consisting of ten pieces of artwork along the Promenade from South Pier. The giant mirror ball, with 46,000 mirrors, is illuminated at night with a colour-changing light show. The artwork *High Tide Organ*, described as a 'musical manifestation of the sea', is one of only a few examples of a tidal organ. The instrument is played by the sea at high tide through eight pipes attached to the sea wall. These are connected under the Promenade to eighteen organ pipes within the sculpture. As the resort 'progresses' into the twenty-first century, the sumptuous banquets, firing of cannons, and impressive processions are a thing of the past, but with over 12 million visitors every year, its success is certainly assured.

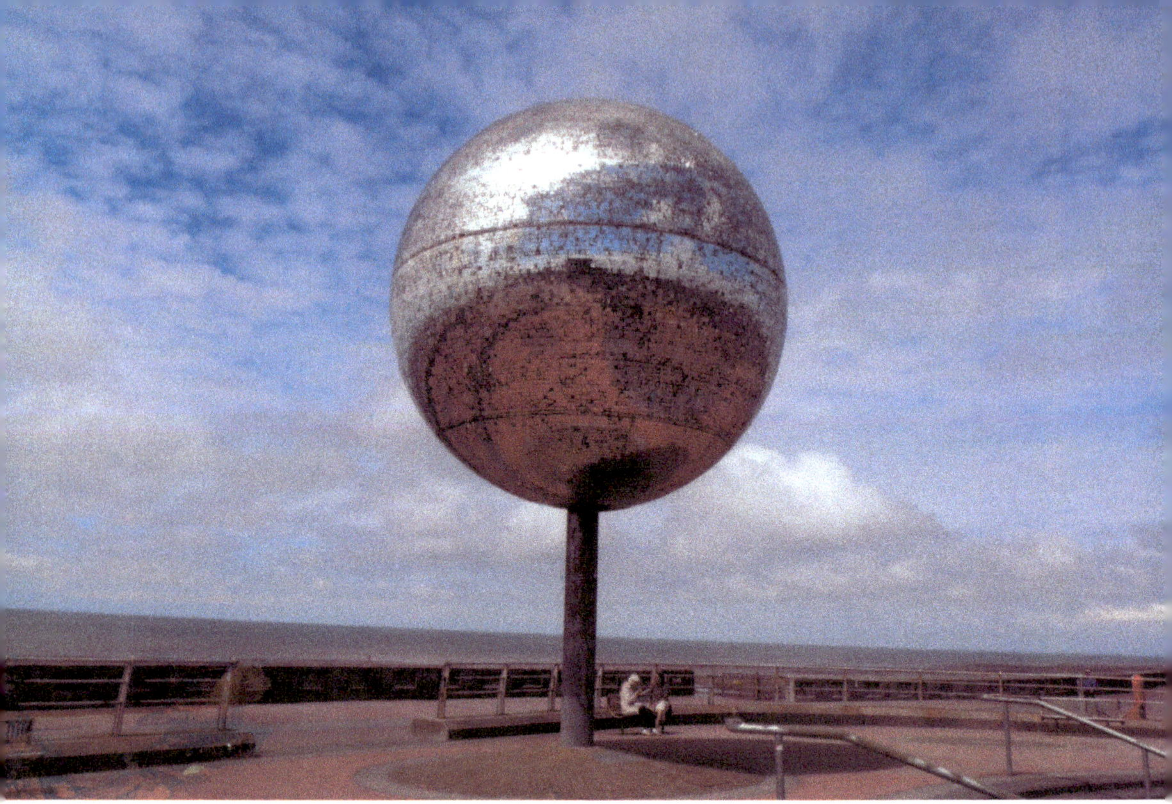

*Above*: World's biggest mirror ball.

*Below*: Sculptures on the Promenade.

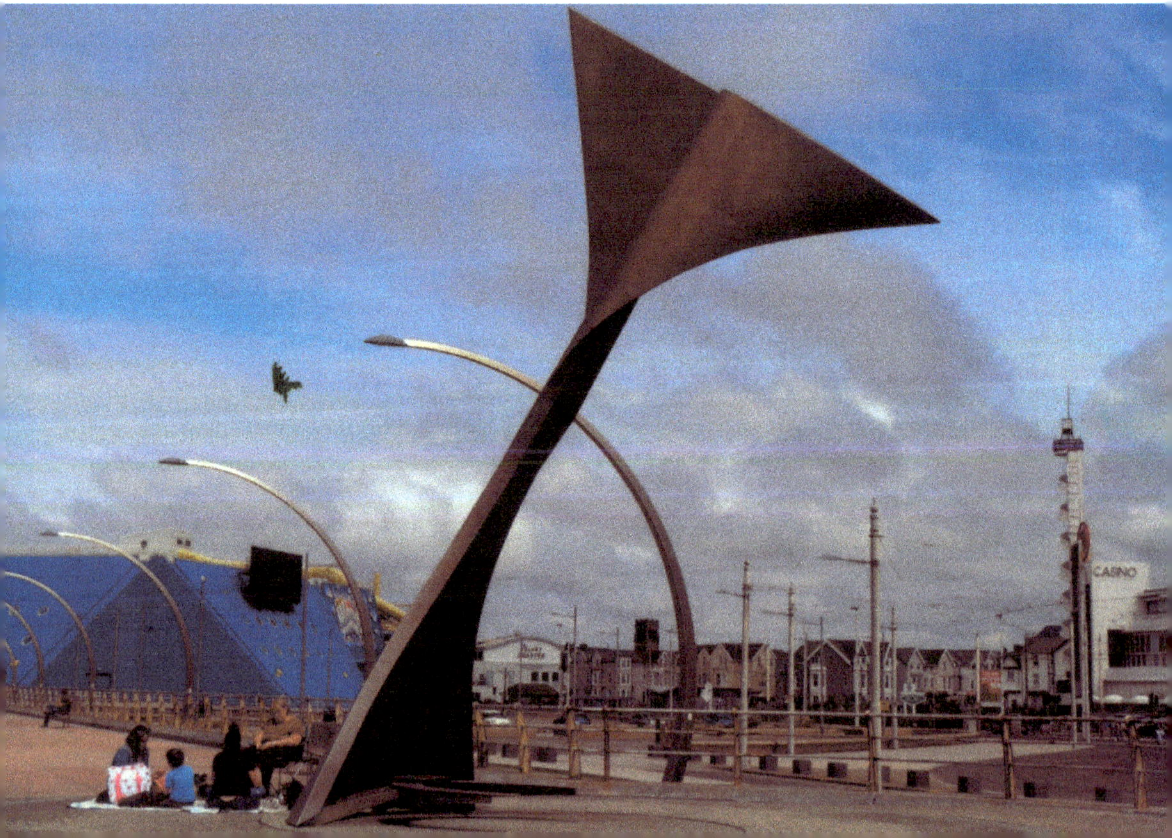

## The Greatest Light Show in the World

Blackpool received the royal seal of approval in 1912, when a gigantic £300,000 scheme of constructing a 3-mile promenade – to be named Princess Parade – was completed. It replaced a narrow iron walkway along the Promenade from South Shore on specially laid railway track. The town was graced by the presence of Princess Louise, daughter of Queen Victoria, accompanied by the Duke of Argyll, who was the principal guest. An estimated 10,000 light bulbs were festooned along the Parade for the opening, and the spectacle of electric light, at a time when most homes were lit with candles and oil lamps, was a revelation to the many visitors who lined the streets to witness this historic event, calling it 'Artificial Sunshine'. The council had devoted the sum of £5,000 to placing eight arc lamps on 60-foot poles in Talbot Square. This proved so popular they were used again six months later, drawing large crowds. This hailed the start of the legendary Blackpool Illuminations.

In 2012, the country celebrated not only the London Olympics and the 100th anniversary of the sinking of the *Titanic*, but also the queen's diamond jubilee. Nearer to home, another significant centenary was celebrated in Blackpool, marking a hundred years since the first official Illuminations were held to commemorate the first royal visit to the town, when Princess Louise came to open a new section of the Promenade between North Pier and Cocker Square.

It was hoped that this would be an annual event, but the outbreak of the First World War meant that it would be another eleven years before the Illuminations

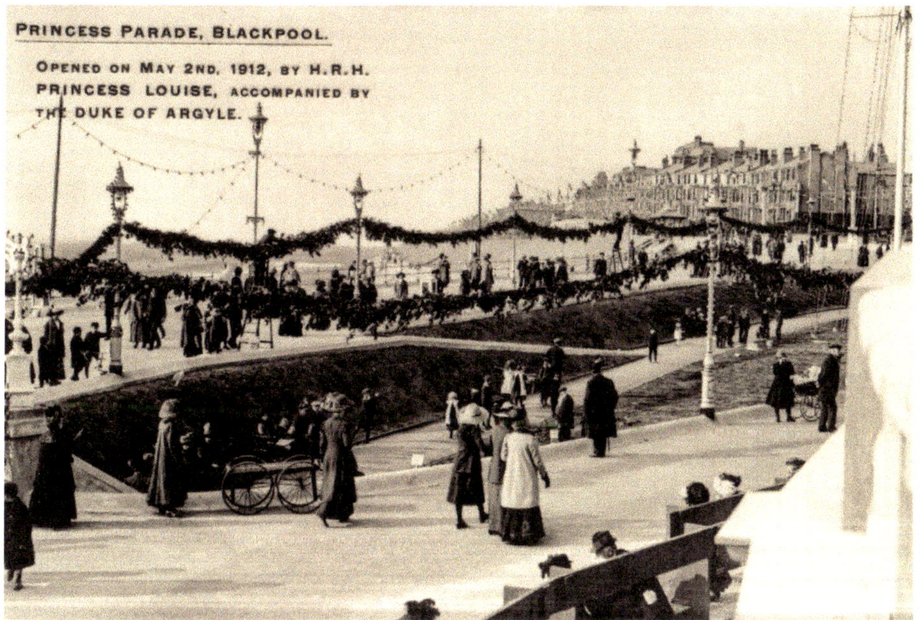


Princess Parade.

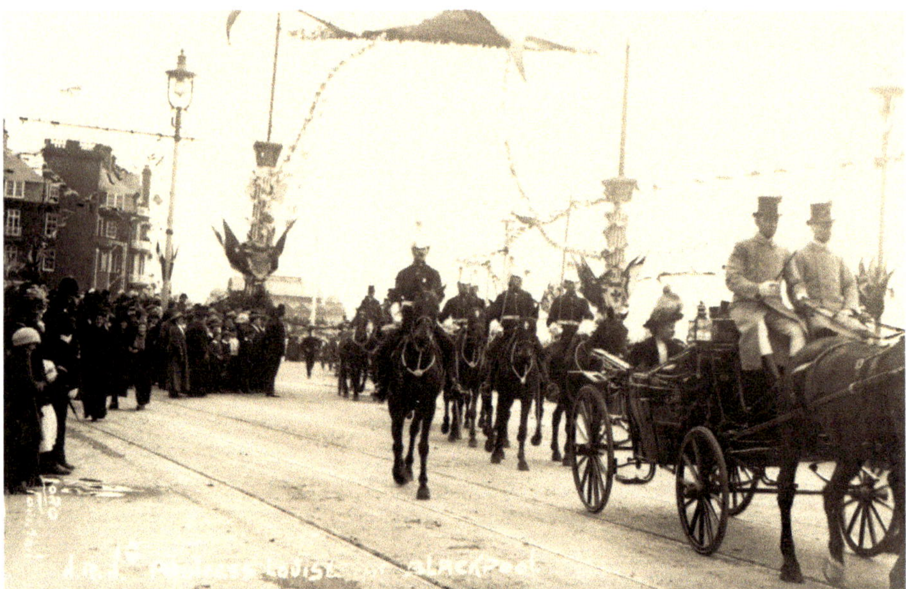



Visit of Princess Louise, 1912.

returned – on 24 October 1925. The lights now stretched from Manchester Square to Cocker Square and several new features had been introduced, including an electric fountain on the seafront and an illuminated gondola tram. A special Jubilee Lifeboat tram was launched in 1926 to celebrate Blackpool's incorporation as a borough. In 1929, it was advertised as 'the greatest spectacle in decorative lighting the world has ever seen'. An amazing number of 300,000 light bulbs were used, and all three piers were lit up for the first time. New lighting innovations from Europe were introduced in the 1930s and a striking tableau depicting children's nursery rhymes was placed on the cliffs while a magnificent peacock, resplendent with coloured lights, dominated the sunken gardens near the Hotel Metropole.

One of the most memorable days in the history of Blackpool was in 1934 when Lord Derby performed the first official switch-on of the Illuminations, to celebrate being made an Honorary Freeman of the Borough, at a ceremony held in the Tower Ballroom. The lights were switched on at 7 p.m., followed by a celebratory banquet. Earlier that day Lord Derby had also laid the foundation stone of the new £60,000 technical college. Over a quarter of a million people lined the seafront, the Illuminations stretching 5 miles along the Promenade. There were 200 excursion trains that had been scheduled to bring visitors to this event, together with 2,200 motor coaches and cars, greatly swelling the number of people.

Five years later, at the outbreak of the Second World War, the lights were dimmed once more and, due to fuel restrictions and lack of finances, they would not return until 1949, when actor Anna Neagle performed the switch-on ceremony. Every year since, the ceremony has been performed by comedians, politicians, athletes,

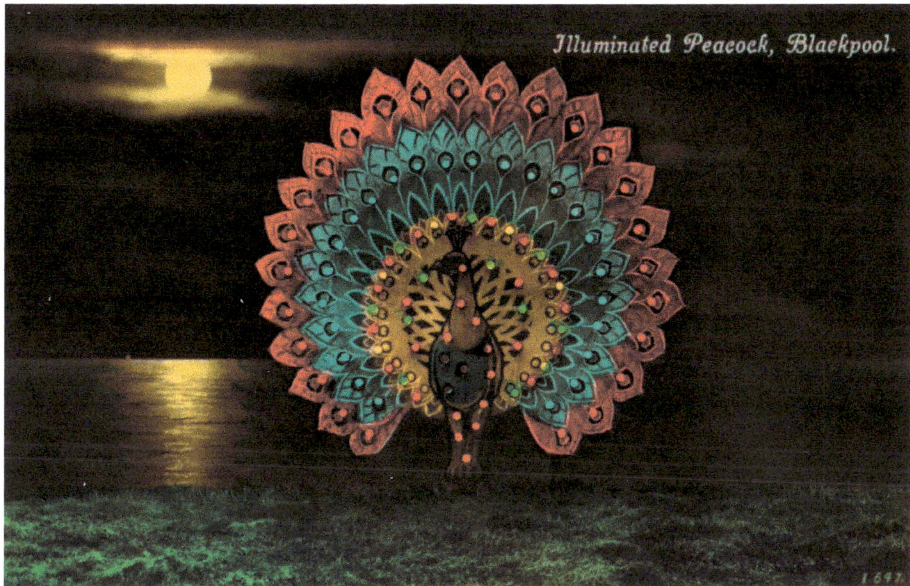



Illuminated peacock.

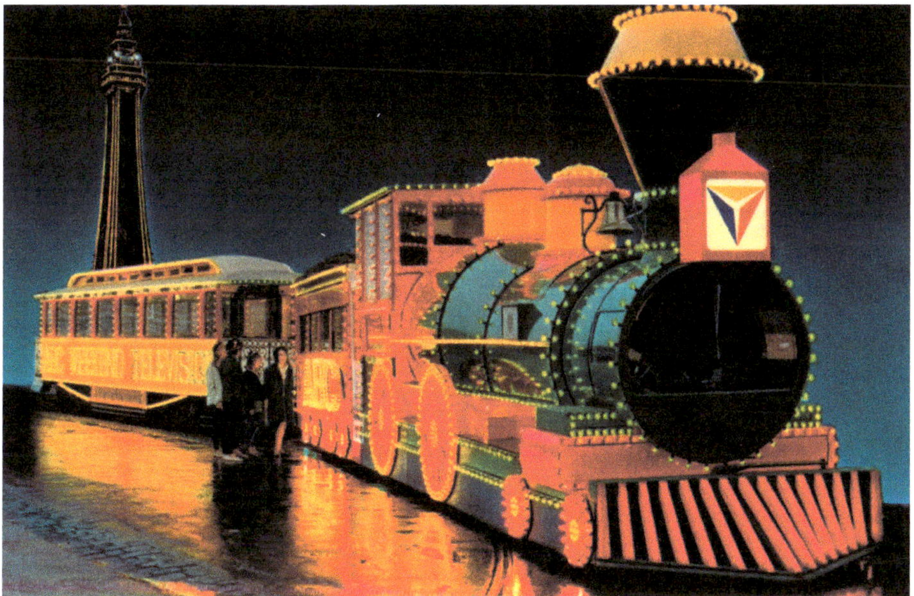

Illuminated train.

and TV and film stars. Two of the most memorable were the 1959 switch on by Jayne Mansfield, and in 1977 when Red Rum was ridden by his jockey through a 'photo finish' style sensor to switch on the lights. The Illuminations continue as an annual event, extending the season into November, and the displays are more spectacular every year. The Tower is lit up in LED lighting, new gateways have

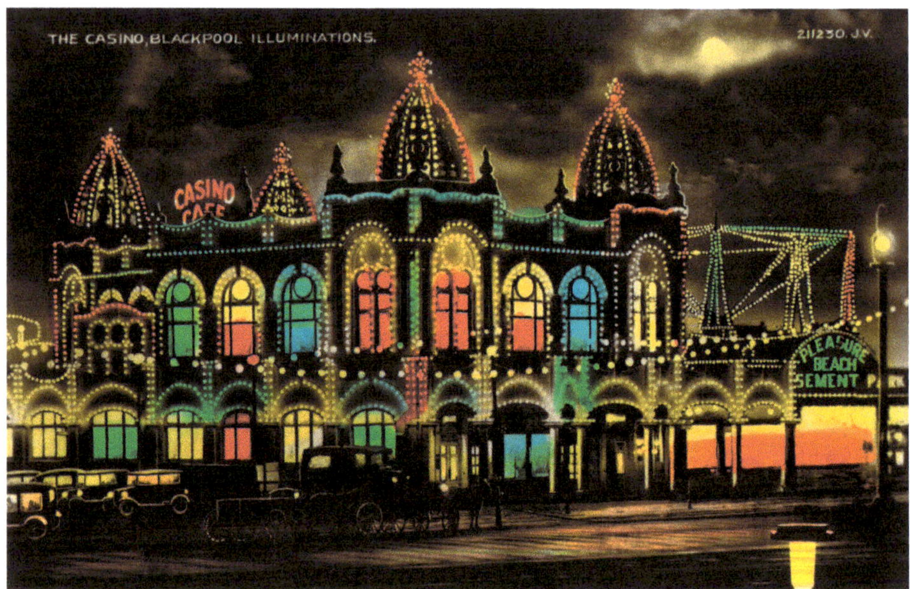

The Casino, Pleasure Beach – Blackpool Illuminations.

been introduced at arrival points in the town, and there is a new artistic light installation at the Grundy Art Gallery. In 2011, cuts were made to the Illumination Fund, but grants from the Government's Coastal Communities, Blackpool Council, and donations from the public have secured their future. In 2012, the centenary year of the Illuminations, the group Friends of the Illuminations was formed, securing the patronage of the celebrity Laurence Llewellyn-Bowen, who has been its creative curator ever since. Another significant centenary was also celebrated in Blackpool, marking 100 years since the first official Illuminations were held to commemorate the first royal visit to the town of Princess Louise.

In 2019, the Illuminations ran from 30 August to 3 November and included the famous Lightpool Festival, held from 11 to 26 October and featuring a convoy of illuminated trams parading along the Promenade. This unique event is vital for the economy of the town.

## Carnival Revels

After the austerities of the war years and temporary cessation of the Illuminations, Blackpool decided to hold a carnival, which they hoped would become an annual event. The carnival proved such a success that it was repeated the following year. The ten-day event started on 11 June with a 2-mile procession of 100 floats, which was watched by 150,000 people. The crowds strained their necks to catch a glimpse of the Carnival King and Queen, the former played by Doodles the Clown from the Tower Circus and the latter by local actor and comedian Fred Walmsley.

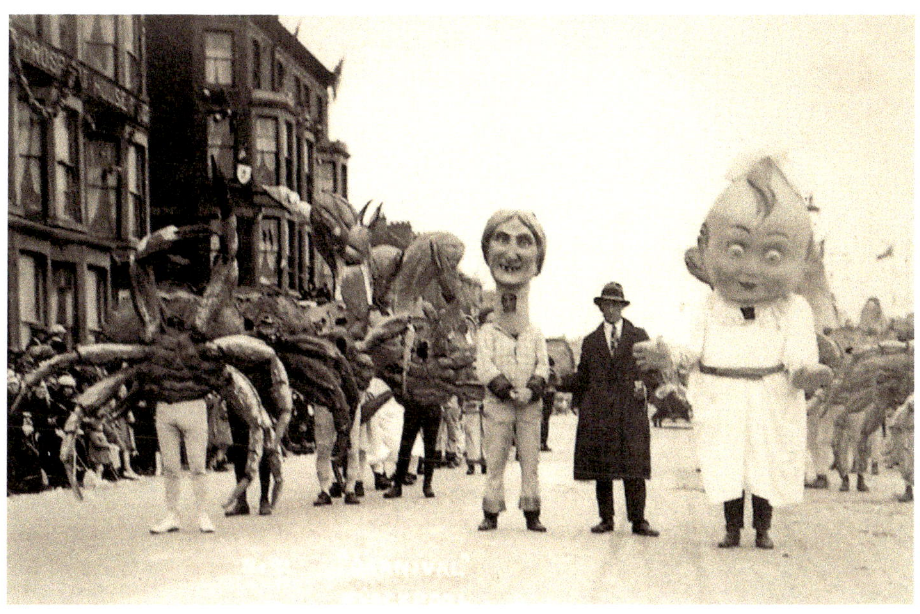

*Above*: Carnival parade.

*Right*: The first Blackpool Carnival, 1923.

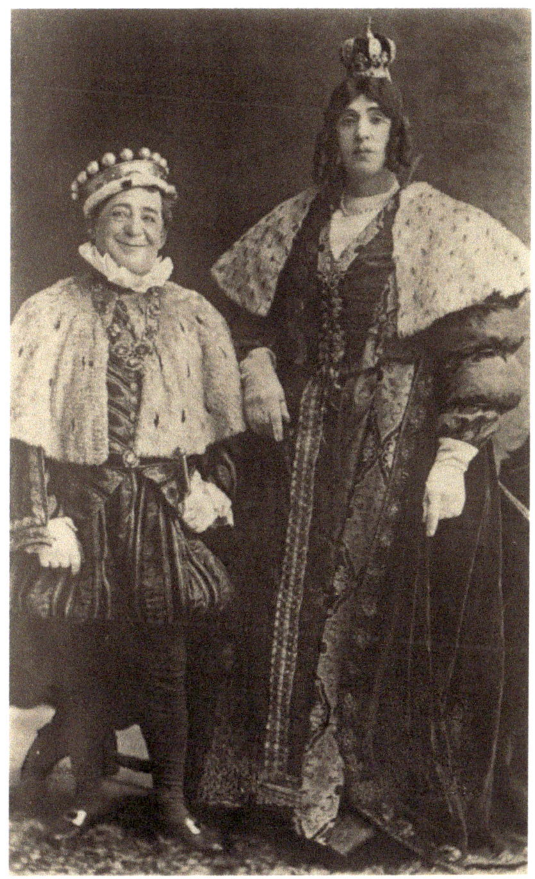

The local press reported that 'Blackpool eclipses all other fetes and is still flying the flag of progress.' The festival was proclaimed a great success, bringing in record numbers of 250,000 people every day for eight days. The seafront was festooned with thousands of flags, and the proceedings served to enhance the reputation of Blackpool as a premier holiday resort.

However, the 1924 carnival was marred by drunken revelry during the week, which put an end to such plans for the next ninety-three years. *The Gazette* said, 'In future it would be better to leave carnivals alone.' Plans were then put in place to reinstate the Illuminations the following year, but after the mid-1920s, Blackpool, like the rest of England, went through a recession. There had been a general strike, and before the economy could recover properly the Second World War was declared in 1939. Consequently, the carnival was largely forgotten – until 2017, when a Blackpool group was awarded £10,000 from the Lottery Fund.

Blackpool Carnival finally achieved its aim of being an annual event, attracting record crowds in 2018 and 2019, and the town enjoyed 'A Carnival with a Jubilee Theme in 2022'. This revival means that a new generation of visitors will be able to enjoy the carnival for the twenty-first century, celebrating the evolving culture of all who now live in Blackpool and the North of England.

# Legends and Heroes of Blackpool

## Seasiders Footballing Icons

The year 1953 was an eventful one for the country, with the conquest of Everest and the coronation of Queen Elizabeth II, but Blackpool had its own reason for rejoicing. The FA Cup final that year was a triumph for Seasiders player Stanley Matthews, who had joined the team in 1947, paving the way for Blackpool's

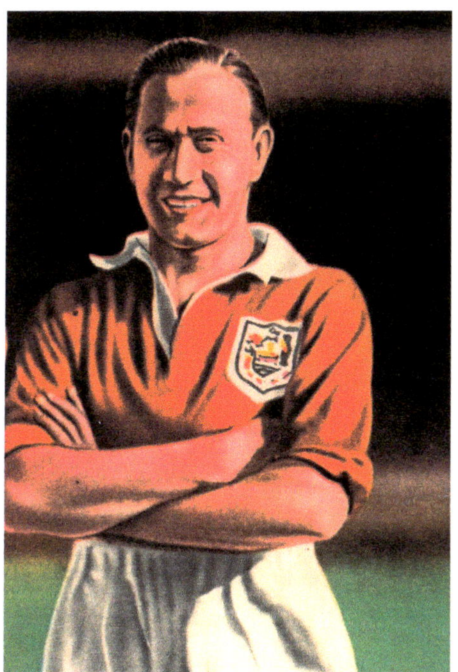

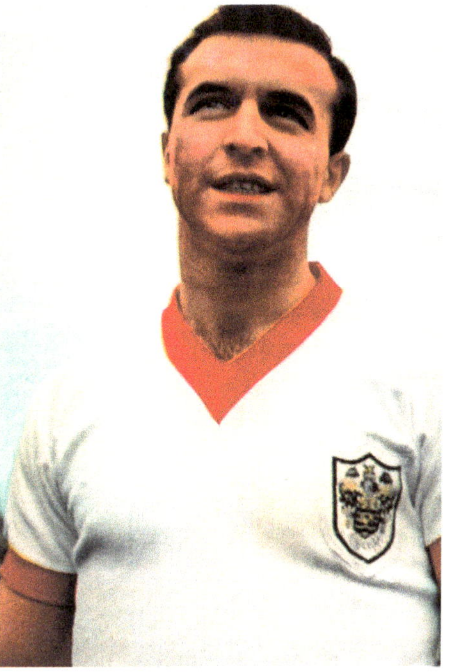

*Above left*: Stan Mortensen.

*Above right*: Jimmy Armfield.

last-minute victory against Bolton Wanderers, when they beat them 4-3 with a winning goal in stoppage time and thereafter known as the 'Matthews Final'.

Stan Mortensen, a native of South Shields, spent fourteen years at Blackpool and, after being on the losing side in the 1948 and 1951 FA Cup finals, became the first and only player to score a hat trick in an FA Cup final at Wembley. After leaving Blackpool to play for other football clubs, he retired from playing on 24 April 1958 at the age of thirty-seven due to injury. He returned to Blackpool as manager between 1967 and 1969, and auctioned his football medals to raise funds for the ailing club. Although he was sacked from his post, he was voted vice president on 20 October 1983 at the annual general meeting of the Blackpool Supporters. On 28 November 1989, he led the Blackpool team out onto the pitch for their FA Cup first-round tie with Bolton Wanderers. On 30 November, a tribute dinner was held at Blackpool's Savoy Hotel to honour his fifty years of service to both Blackpool Football Club and the town.

To celebrate the best players in the club's history, the Seasiders Hall of Fame – situated inside the concourse in the north-west corner of Bloomfield Road Football Ground – was officially opened on 22 August 2006. The Blackpool Supporters Association asked fans to vote for their all-time heroes, and five players from each decade up to the 1990s were inducted. The first to be inducted was former Blackpool Football Club and England captain Jimmy Armfield, who is commemorated by a blue plaque, which was unveiled at Revoe Learning Academy by Blackpool Civic Trust.

A civic reception was held for Jimmy to celebrate his seventieth birthday and a tangerine flag was flown from the Town Hall for the day in his honour. Having played hundreds of times for the Seasiders, a stand was dedicated to him at Bloomfield Road in 2010, and a new secondary school was named after him in 2017. In 2003, he had been awarded the Freedom of Blackpool, alongside the Pleasure Beach chairman, Mrs Doris Thompson. Following his death on 22 January 2018, hundreds turned up to Bloomfield Road on 8 February, as his funeral cortege passed through the football stadium before he was laid to rest at a private service at St Peter's Church. People had been arriving all morning, some laying floral tributes on his statue. At noon, the funeral procession entered the ground, travelling down one touchline before pausing briefly in front of the stand that had been named after him.

## A Little Bit of Blackpool Rock

Blackpool has been making and selling rock for over a hundred years, ever since a Yorkshireman called Ben Bullock made the first batch and sent it to the rapidly growing resort to tempt the holidaymakers. George Seniors was possibly the first person to make Blackpool rock in the town in 1902 and founded Star Confectionery Company, on Bank Hey Road, where the public could watch the sweets being made. It was also sold from stalls on the beach and, although illegal, hawkers sold rock from baskets in the streets with a lookout to warn of any policemen approaching. One well-known rock vendor was Billy Muggins. Instantly recognisable by his top hat and clogs, he who would throw out sticks of rock to attract a crowd before he started his sales patter.

In the 1920s many more confectionery manufacturers sprung up in Blackpool, such as Waller and Hartley, Newsome's (who could be seen demonstrating rock making on the Pleasure Beach), and the Coronation Rock Company started by Alex Bolton in 1927, which is still operating today under the name of Coronation Candy.

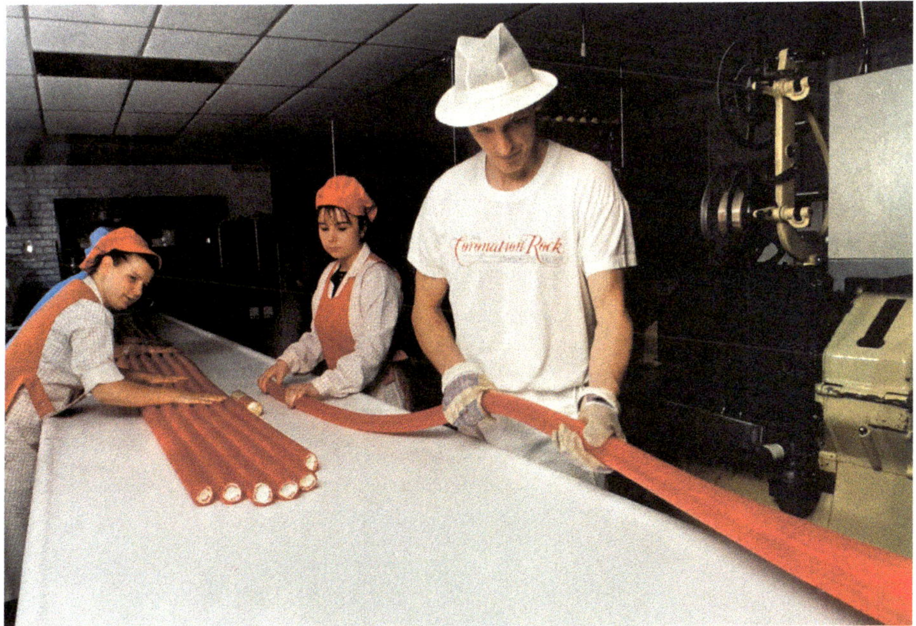

*Above*: Workers at Coronation Rock.

*Right*: Rock seller on the front at Blackpool.

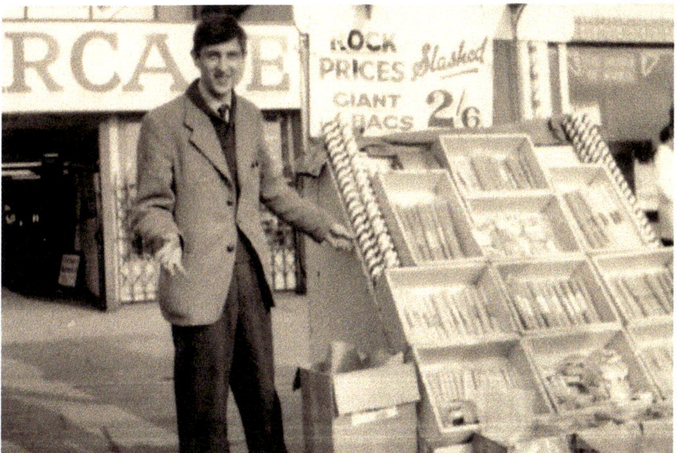

The Coronation Rock Company traditionally makes a presentation stick of rock for each celebrity selected to switch on the Illuminations. They also hold the record for making the world's biggest stick of rock, measuring 4.49 metres long and weighing nearly 70 stones.

## Roma and Travellers – a Long and Colourful History

People from the traveller community have a long history in Blackpool, dating to around 1810 when, according to Kathleen Eyre in her book *Seven Golden Miles*, the first significant settlement was on the clifftops at North Shore, situated near the Gynn public house and Uncle Tom's Cabin. Known then as 'gypsies', their fortune-telling tents and booths drew many visitors, until they were forced to move when the cliffs began to erode. In the 1830s an encampment began to develop on the sandhills to the south of the town. The arrival from the south-east of England of perhaps the most well-known gypsy couple, Edward (Ned) and Sarah Boswell, was the start of a dynasty, whose name began to appear on notices around their tent, immortalised in numerous Edwardian postcards. Edward and Sarah were followed over the coming years by other families such as Lees, Boswells, Youngs, Townsends, and Smiths. At the turn of the twentieth century, South Shore was home to twenty-one sets of families. Ten of them paid £20 –25 to pitch their tents and a further 12s 6d for access to the water supply.

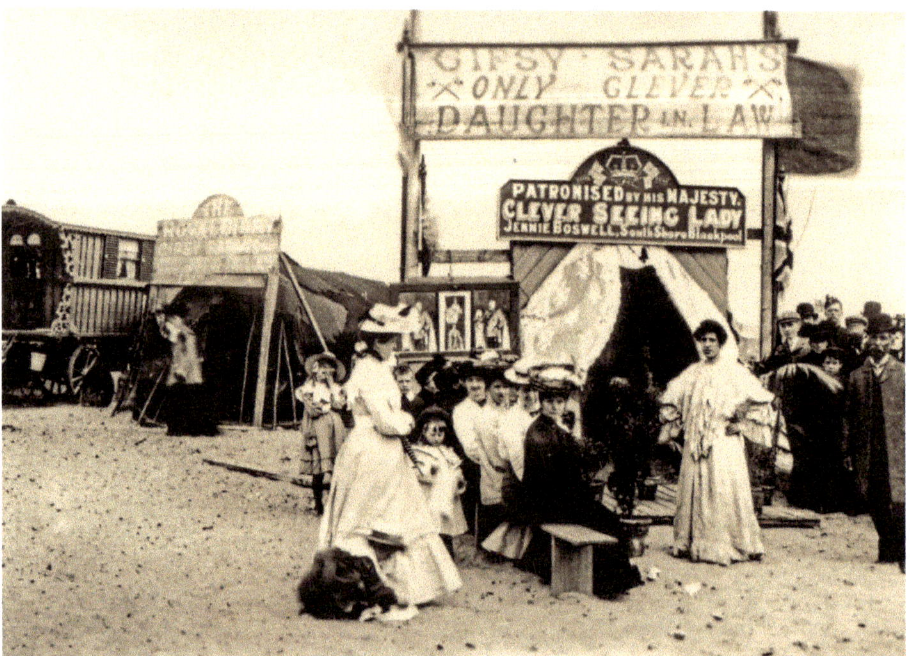


Ladies waiting to have their fortunes told.

## Sarah Boswell, the All-seeing Lady

The number of gypsies swelled each summer by visiting gypsies from all over the country, catering for the expanding holiday trade. The women told fortunes, while the men operated shooting galleries, merry-go-rounds, switchback railways and other mechanical rides. In the winter months they kept themselves occupied by weaving baskets, hawking and scissor grinding. Edward (Ned) and Sarah Boswell, being the founder members of the encampment, were practically regarded as Romany aristocracy and claimed to be the only family of true Roma blood. Sarah claimed to have second sight and told the fortunes of thousands of visitors over her long life. She died in 1904 at the age of ninety-nine in her isolated home – a canvas tent that she had steadfastly refused to move from. She had brought up nine children there and had countless descendants. Many of the gypsies claimed a relationship with Sarah, and the postcard here advertises Jennie Boswell 'Gypsy Sarah's only clever daughter in law', 'Patronised by His Majesty' the 'Clever Seeing Lady'.

Her daughter, Ada Boswell, was known as 'Queen of the Gypsies', a title claimed to have been bestowed upon her by Queen Victoria, to whom she was the official palm reader. Fortune tellers were in great demand in Victorian times. Each summer the queue outside her tent stretched for miles as day-trippers and holidaymakers waited to discover what fate had in store for them. On Ada's death in 1901, the mantle passed to her granddaughter, Daisy Boswell, who was summoned to court in 1909 for the crime of 'pretending to tell fortunes'. After failing to appear at court she was sentenced to 'two weeks and two months' imprisonment with hard labour for the current offence, with an additional fourteen days for a previous offence.

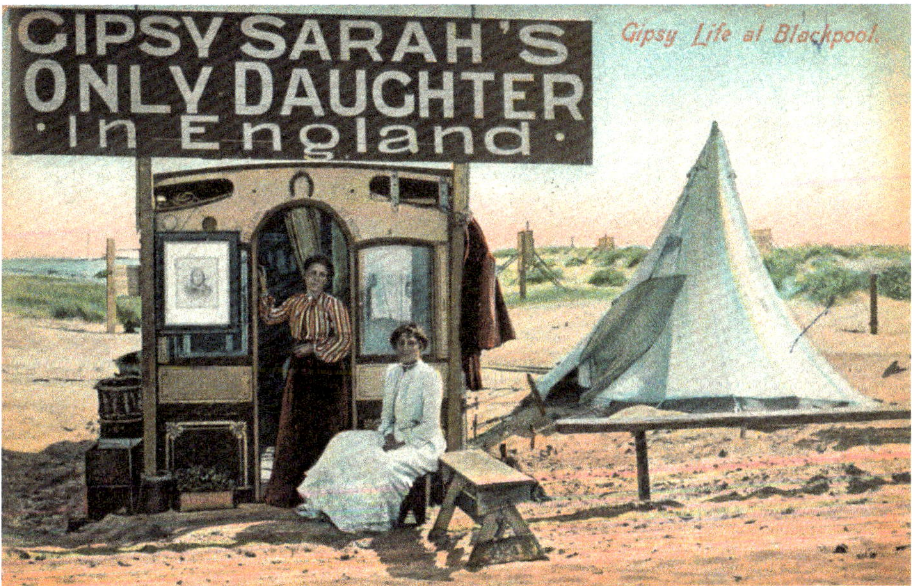


'Gypsy Life at Blackpool.'

Although the Boswells had often fallen foul of the law, by the time of Sarah Boswell's death in 1904 they were looked upon as one of the area's most respected families, as was borne out by Councillor Harrison, who, when addressing a meeting of the town's council paid tribute to the family for obeying the town's bylaws. She was mourned by not just the gypsy community and her family, but by the thousands of people who had included a visit to her as part of their holiday itinerary. She was so old that she remembered when Blackpool had only thirty or forty houses. Edward ('Ned') and Sarah are commemorated on a gravestone at Layton Cemetery.

The gypsy community had always been a positive asset to the tourist trade, but this was to change when the Pleasure Beach was being developed. In 1908, Blackpool Corporation decided to prohibit all fortune telling, phrenology, and palmists on the beach, but gypsies could remain if they gave up 'palm tickling'. As this was their main source of income, the practice of fortune telling persisted and, in 1909 four women were charged at Blackpool Police Court for 'pretending to tell fortunes'. Eviction notices were finally served on the grounds of sanitation, but it was not until 1910 that the last of them left, the Boswells among the last to leave. Some went to live in houses in Blackpool or Preston, returning to the town in the summer season to ply their trade.

Gypsies continued to have a long and colourful history in Blackpool. In the 1950s one of the most famous was 'Gypsy Rosalee' on the Golden Mile, who was popular with visiting celebrities. Her booth was decorated with photographs of stars for whom she had foretold future success. The tradition still operates today by generations of the Petulengro family, whose surname is the Romani name for Smith, and who descend from one of the oldest known families of palmists and astrologers in the world. Leah Petulengro and her daughter Sarah still operate on the Promenade and North Pier, respectively. Another of the present generations of the family carrying on the family business is Lee Petulengro, grandson of 'Gypsy Rosalee'. The name of Boswell still carries on in Marton Moss, where Tommy Boswell moved from Bury, and whose family live on a new travellers' site there.

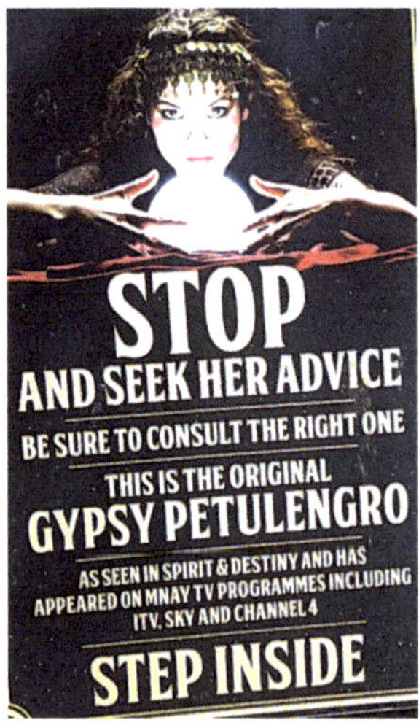



Poster advertising 'Gypsy Petulengro'.

# 4

# The Transport Revolution

## The Railway Comes to Blackpool

The most significant event to contribute to the accessibility of the resort to the masses was the opening of the branch railway on Easter Monday in 1846. At that time the rail network in Britain was rapidly expanding, and this important event was celebrated with great aplomb. Early in the morning, the inhabitants of the town awoke to the sound of cannons firing and the houses, inns, churches, and railway station were festooned with flags and bunting. During the day, trains passed to and from the station at Poulton-le-Fylde, giving free rides. The opening train carried the directors and shareholders of the railway company along with local dignitaries. As the day had been observed as a public holiday, all along the line large numbers of spectators cheered and waved as the trains passed.

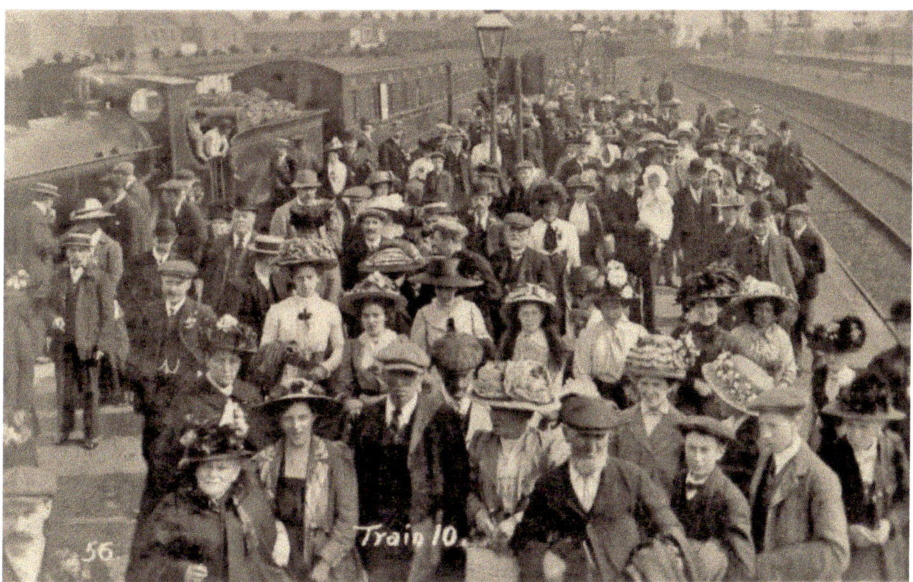

Trippers arriving at Talbot Road railway station, 1911.

Processions of Sunday school children lined the beach and the streets, which were adorned with flags and banners. Children were treated to tea and buns on the bowling green of the Talbot Arms and music was provided by the bands of Rochdale and Preston, the Church of England, and the Bluecoat school. A gala dinner was held at the Clifton Arms for 150 people, including the shareholders of the railway and members of the council. Over forty workers were given a 'good old English dinner with plentiful libations of home brewed ale' at the Talbot Hotel, presided over by the contractor, Mr Jardine.

The new railway station had been simply named Blackpool station, but in 1872 it was renamed Blackpool Talbot Road, changing to its present name Blackpool North station in 1932. It was rebuilt in 1898 with an imposing canopied entrance and a clock tower. In 1974, it was demolished and replaced with a modern building on the site of the former excursion platforms. It now serves as Blackpool's main station.

The second coastal line, running from Blackpool to Lytham, was opened on 6 April and a new station was built called Hounds Hill station, changing to Central station in 1878. The press reported: 'Blackpool and Lytham Railway opened on Monday with considerable ceremony. An "elegant" luncheon was held at the Clifton Arms Hotel, where guests of Colonel Clifton congratulated the Chairman. There were several glasses raised; one of the toasts was "Success to the Railway".'

The opening of this centrally located station cleared the way for even more day-trippers from the surrounding towns and cities. In 1901, the station was enlarged to fourteen platforms, and in 1911 was hailed as the world's busiest railway station. Plans to replace the station in 1938 and 1956 never materialised

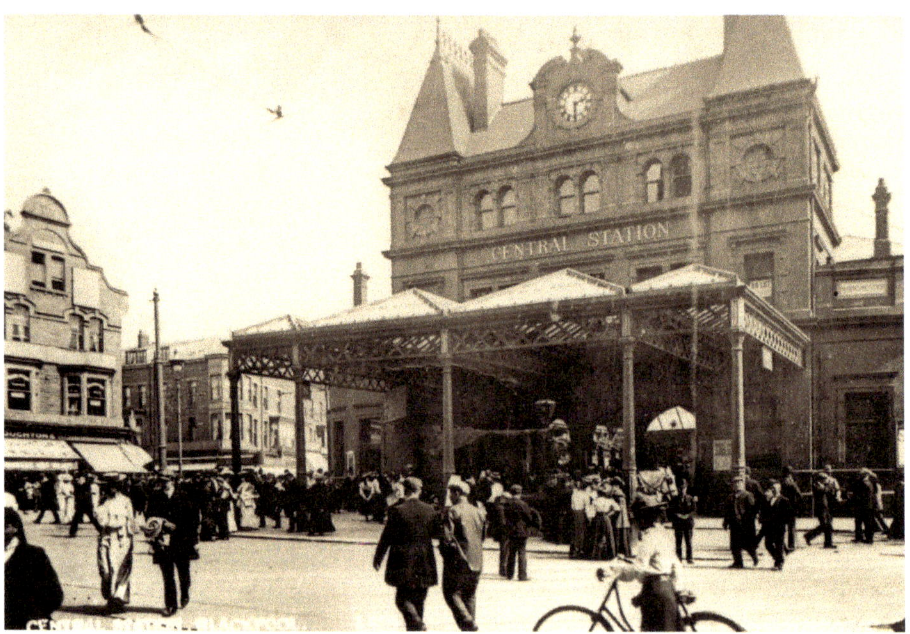


Blackpool Central station.

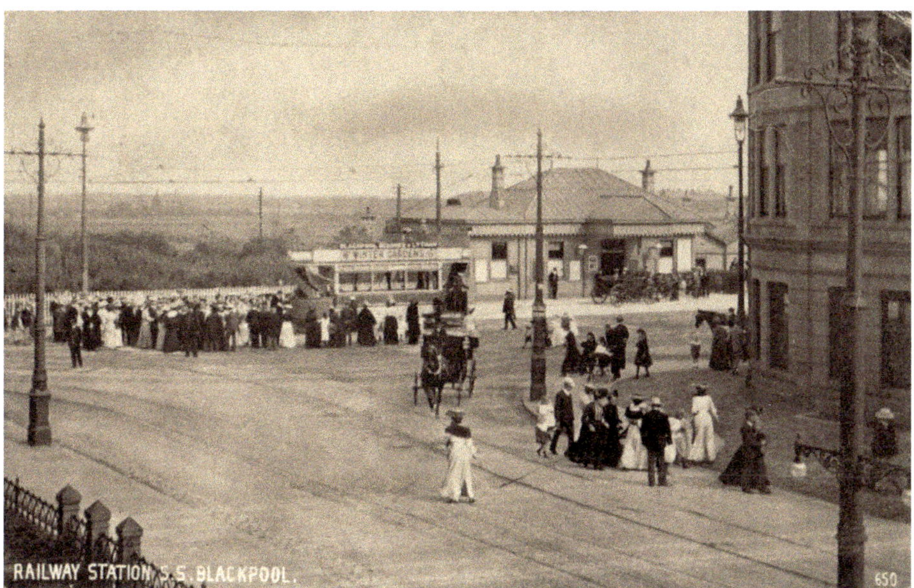



South Shore railway station.

and in 1964, as part of the Beeching cuts, it was finally closed on 2 November and demolished in 1973. It was a surprising decision to close down a terminus more than a century old, which had brought in millions to the heart of the town. The Coral Island Amusement Arcade now stands on the site of the former ticket office and the areas between the platforms have been filled in to create a large car park.

The opening of a new line from Kirkham to South Shore led to the building of a third railway station in 1903, named Waterloo Road. It had only four platforms and, until 1964, was directly connected to Central station. The *Lancashire Evening Post* of 29 May 1903 reported on the opening, saying that it should be a record year for Blackpool with new, additional places of amusement, a skating rink, new pavilions to the North and Central piers, and the widening of the Promenade.

With the closing of Central station in 1964, Blackpool South (as it was renamed on 17 March 1932) went into decline, but visitors continued to come from all over the country. In 1967, a day excursion by coach from Derby to Blackpool cost 21*s* and a visit to the Illuminations was the same price – a bargain indeed.

## Three Centuries of Blackpool Trams

In the late 1800s the UK's first electric tram service officially opened on 29 September 1885. Its official opening was celebrated at the same time as the launch of the new lifeboat, the *Samuel Fletcher*. The mayors of Liverpool and Manchester started the train on the electric tramway, followed by sporting activities, a contest of band music, and a ball at the Raikes Hotel. The two main dignitaries of Blackpool, Alderman Cocker and Councillor Bickerstaffe, were joined by the chief municipal officers of thirty northern towns who followed the Grand Lifeboat procession before four lifeboats were launched at South Pier. The festivities concluded with a firework display and a banquet at the Town Hall.

The 1930s saw the introduction of a fleet of modern, streamlined trams that were to form the backbone of the fleet into the twenty-first century. By the 1950s a total of 150 trams were operating, transporting 45 million passengers every year on various routes. The Railcoach tram pictured was manufactured in Loughborough in 1937 with luxurious interiors and a sliding sunshine roof. A few remained in use until the £100 million upgrade of the tramway in 2012, when the old heritage vehicles were replaced by a fleet of sixteen new Bombadier Flexity trams. Some of the vintage trams still operate for tourists.

On the centenary of the tram service in 1985 the *Illustrated London News* of 1 September reported that 'Blackpool was the first town to have an electric street railway and the last to retain its trams long enough to celebrate their centenary year.' In 1998, the centenary of the Blackpool to Fleetwood tramway was commemorated by a week-long event involving a parade of historically important trams in the history of the tramway. To celebrate the 125th anniversary, a cavalcade of vintage trams, some dating back to 1898, operated a one-hour return trip 9 miles along the coast to Fleetwood. Seven Illumination tours took place, and the town was packed with tram enthusiasts.

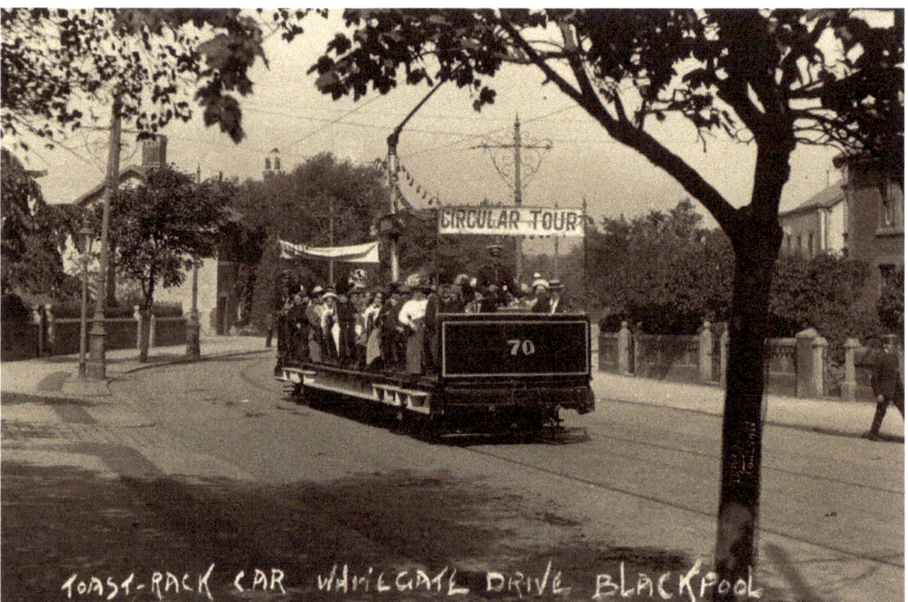


One of the popular toast-rack trams, of which thirty were built from 1911. They carried sixty-nine passengers, spread out over fourteen benches, on a circular tour around the resort and operated until the beginning of the Second World War, when they were taken out of service.

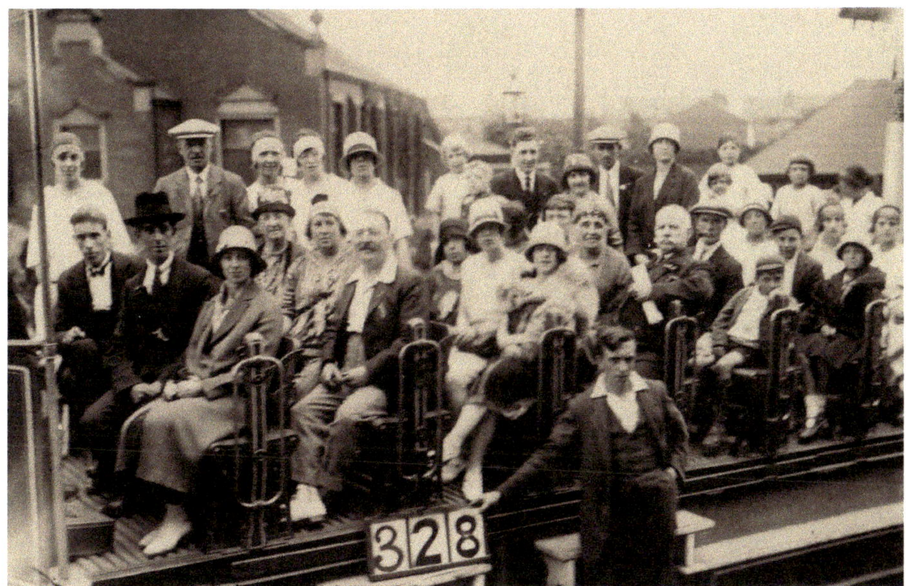

Passengers enjoying a tram ride.

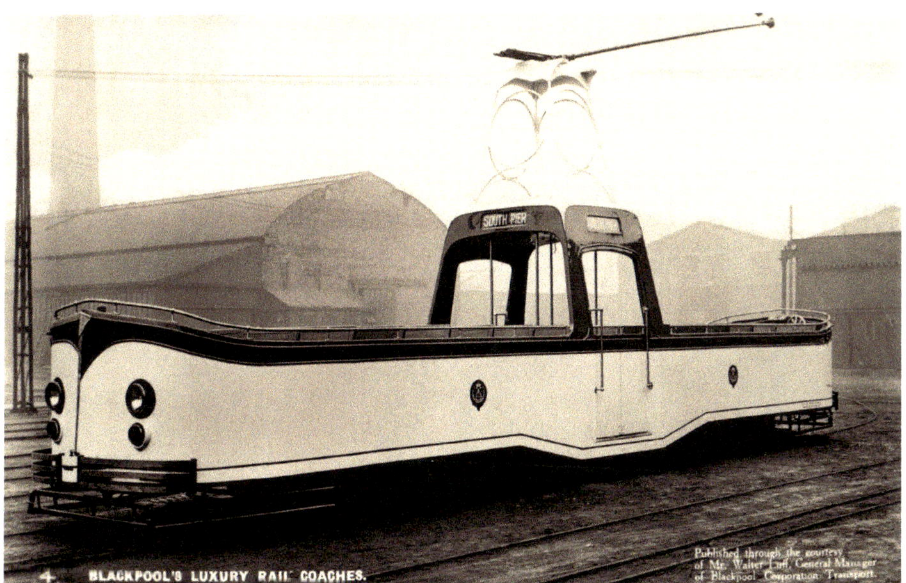



Railcoach tram.

As part of the major works in 2012, a new tram depot was erected at Starr
Gate and 11 kilometres of track was replaced. The official opening ceremony
was performed by the UK Transport Minister, Norman Baker, who, together with
invited guests – forty passengers who had won a competition – were the first to
take the day's historic journey from Blackpool Tower to Fleetwood on the new
state-of-the-art trams.

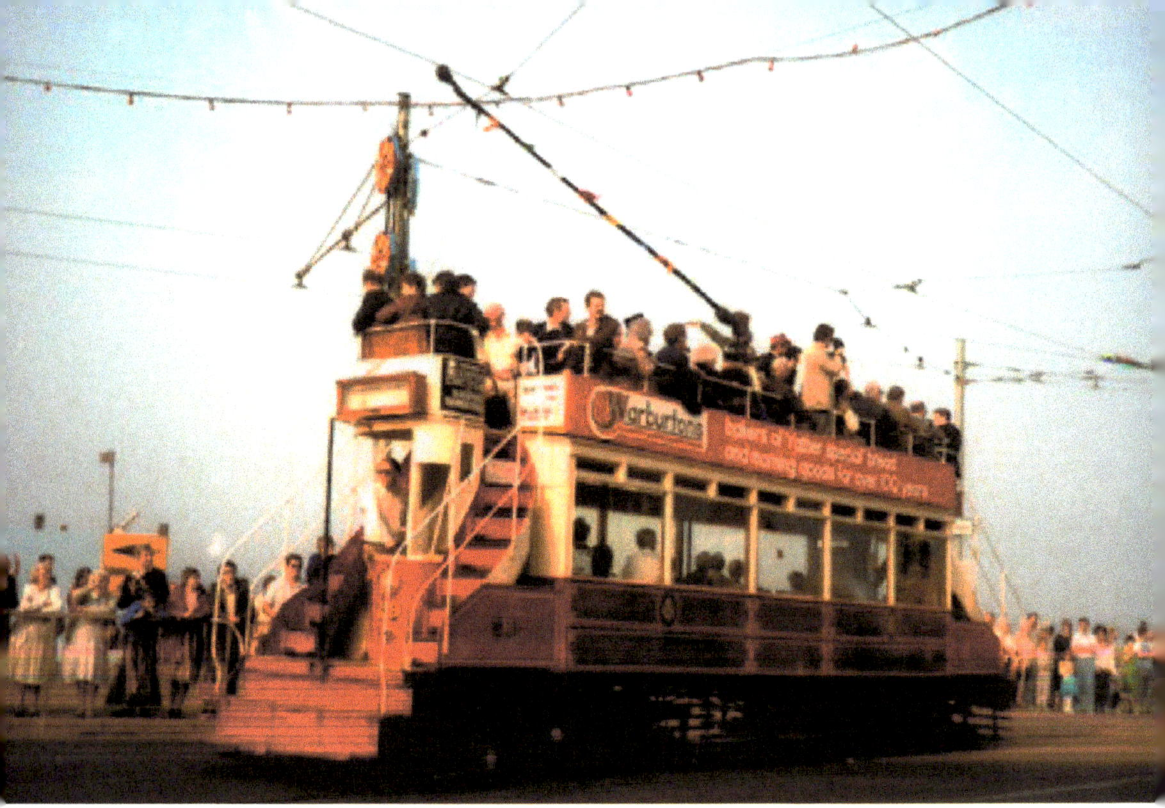

*Above*: Centenary tram, 1985.

*Below*: Tram on its way to Starr Gate.

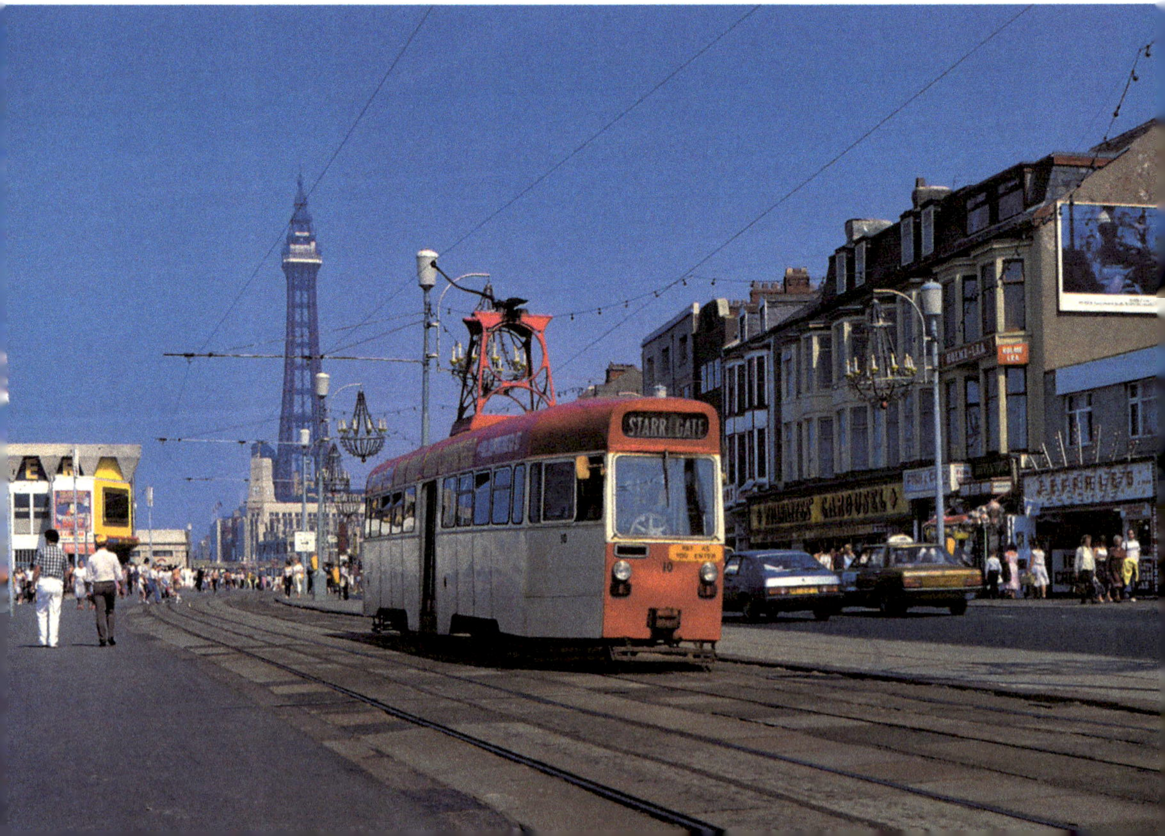

Further work is in progress to extend the tramway up Talbot Road, from North Pier to Blackpool North railway station as part of an ongoing project to improve the town centre. On the site of the demolished Wilko store on Talbot Road a new tram terminus and hotel are being constructed. Blackpool Transport is buying two new trams in time for the opening of the new link, bringing its fleet to eighteen. To celebrate Blackpool's special tram heritage, the latest development in preparation for the new link is the installation of two new stainless-steel benches, with a design inspired from the heritage trams, situated in Talbot Square. They are located near to where the tram stop will be once trams run between North Pier and North station and have been funded by a grant from the Lancashire Enterprise Partnership.

# 5

# The Entertainment Capital of the World

## Grand Palaces of Pleasure

Most of the significant attractions in Blackpool were developed in the second half of the nineteenth century. The construction of the first two of the resort's piers was followed by the opening of the Raikes Hall Pleasure Gardens in 1872. This magnificent 40-acre complex soon developed into a major attraction, which included a large boating lake, conservatory surrounded by terraces, meandering footpaths, and flowerbeds. Its main features were a racing track, dancing

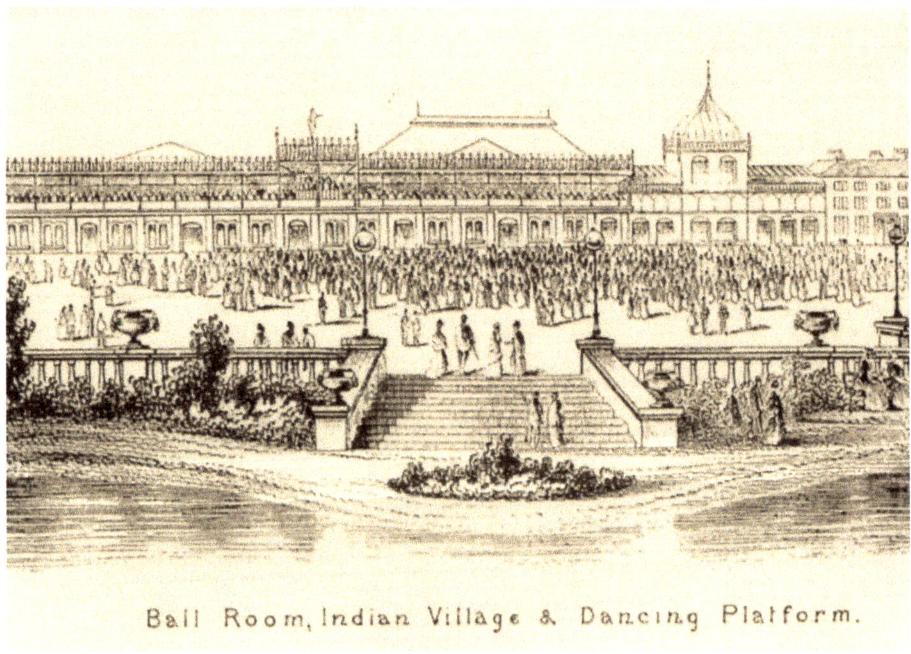


Ballroom, Indian Village and dancing platform.

platforms, a monkey house and aviary, ballroom, a theatre, and a switchback. For twenty years it thrived as the premier place of entertainment, but the new attractions of the Tower, Alhambra, and Grand Theatre nearer to the town centre meant that the site lost popularity and eventually fell derelict. The extensive Pleasure Gardens finally closed in 1901, and the name is preserved in the only surviving building, the Raikes Hall public house.

The design of places of entertainment, such as ballrooms and theatres, in the Victorian era was often influenced by Indian palaces, starting with the Pavilion at Brighton in the late eighteenth century. The magnificent Alhambra (pictured here next to Blackpool Tower with its 3,000-seat theatre, 3,000-capacity ballroom, and 2,000-seat circus) was a financial disaster due to competing with attractions at the Tower and only operated from 1899 to 1903. It was reopened in 1904 as the Palace, the interior having been redesigned by Frank Matcham, the famous theatre designer. Blackpool lost one of its design masterpieces when it was tragically demolished in 1961, to be replaced by modern buildings of no architectural merit.

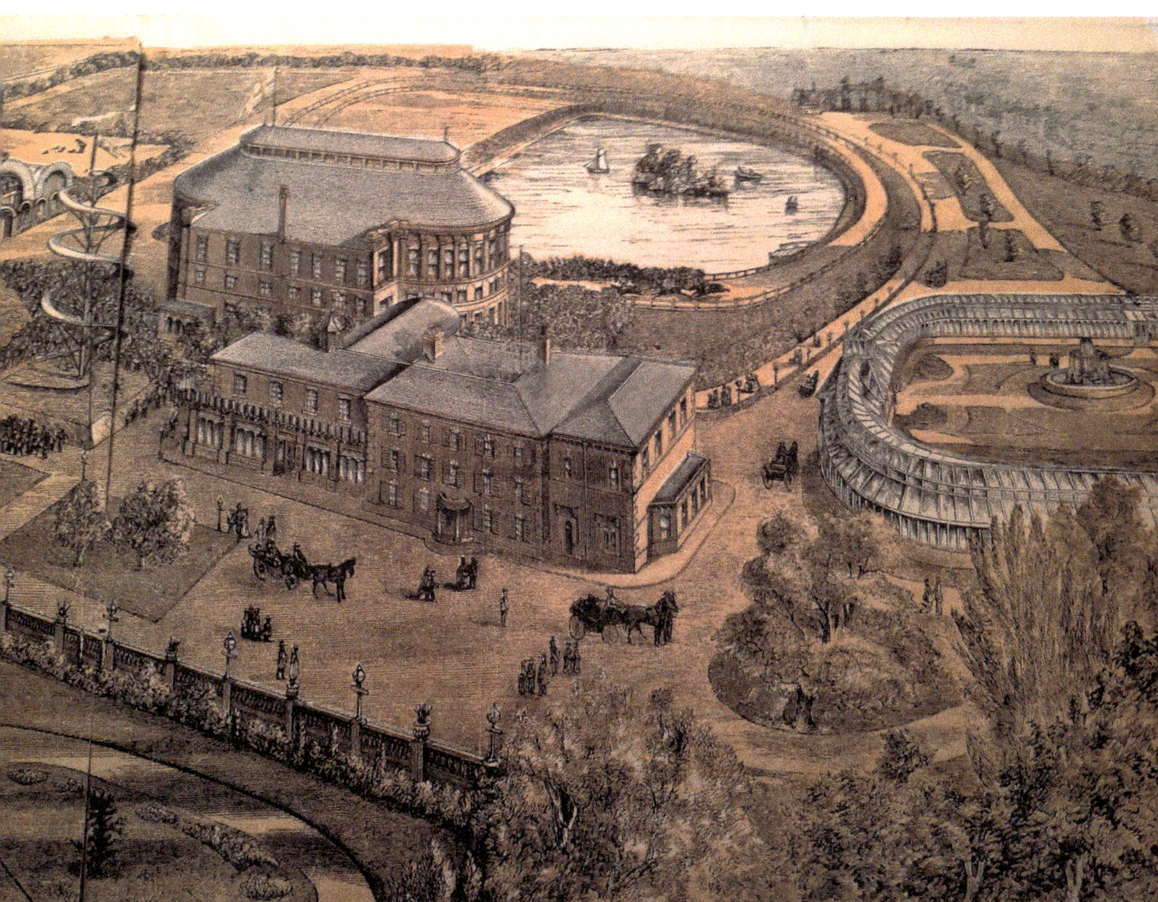

Raikes Hall Pleasure Gardens.

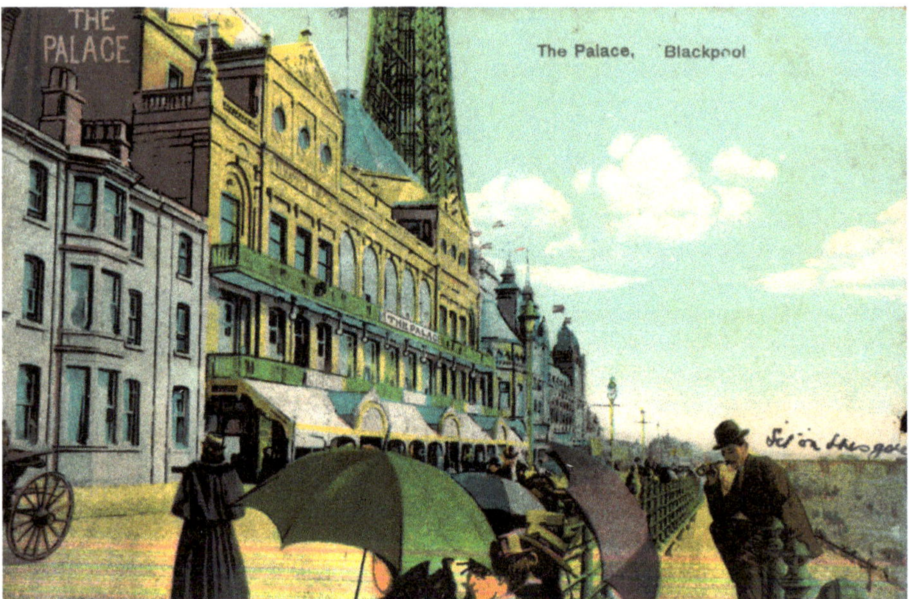

The Palace, Promenade.

## Ballrooms of Romance

Some of the most ornate and stylish ballrooms sprang up in British seaside resorts in
the Victorian age, the most famous of which is the Tower Ballroom, which opened
in 1894. It is world famous for its unique spring dance floor and has outlasted any
other ballroom in the country. The perfect locale for dancing to the sounds of the
Wurlitzer or watching from the side lines while enjoying afternoon tea.

After its completion it was soon enlarged and remodelled by Frank Matcham,
the leading theatre architect of the day. It was a masterpiece of design, with its
elaborate gilded plasterwork, frescoes, cherubs, pillars, and sprung parquet floor.
A major catastrophe occurred in 1956 when the ballroom suffered a devastating
fire, leaving it a charred ruin. Thanks to the efforts of the ballroom's art director,
Andrew Mazzio, it was lovingly restored, and the reopening ceremony was
performed on 22 May by Douglas Bickerstaffe. In 2022, the much-loved ballroom
underwent a massive £1.1 million refurbishment, lasting over six months, to
restore the famous venue to its original glory. It has outlasted every other ballroom
in the country, and, in addition to hosting dance championships, it is also now
famous for hosting the TV show *Strictly Come Dancing* for one weekend every
year, when to 'make it to Blackpool' is the ambition of every competitor.

A major contributor to the success of the Tower Ballroom over the years was
the talented organist Reginald Dixon, who entertained holidaymakers for over
forty years by playing his mighty Wurlitzer, which rose from beneath the stage
in the ballroom. He was lovingly known as 'Mr Blackpool' until he played his

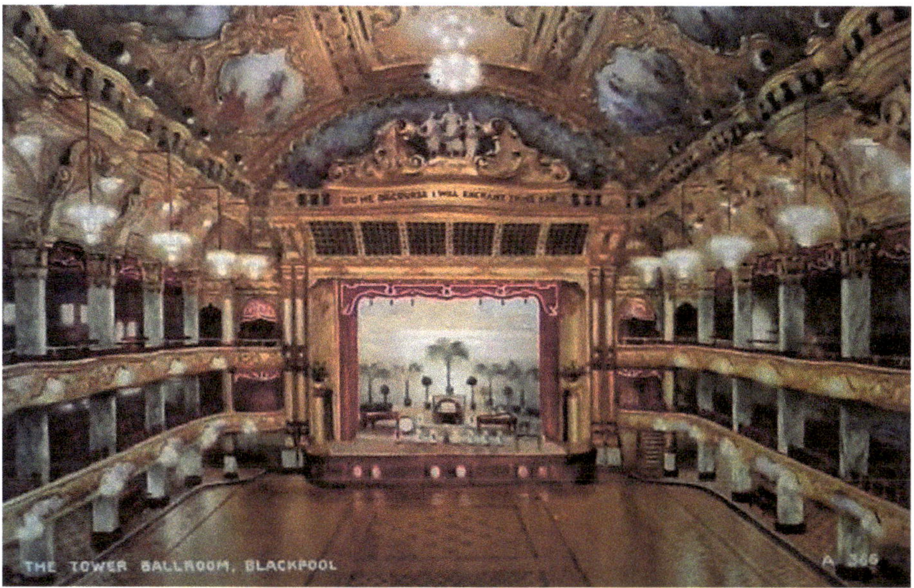

The Tower Ballroom.

farewell performance on 29 March 1979, ending a long and successful association with the Tower. Famous for his radio broadcasts and record sales, his famous signature tune 'I Do Like to be Beside the Seaside' was first played in 1931.

After the success of the Tower Ballroom, in 1896 the Winter Gardens followed with its own ballroom, the Empress, whose main entrance was through the newly

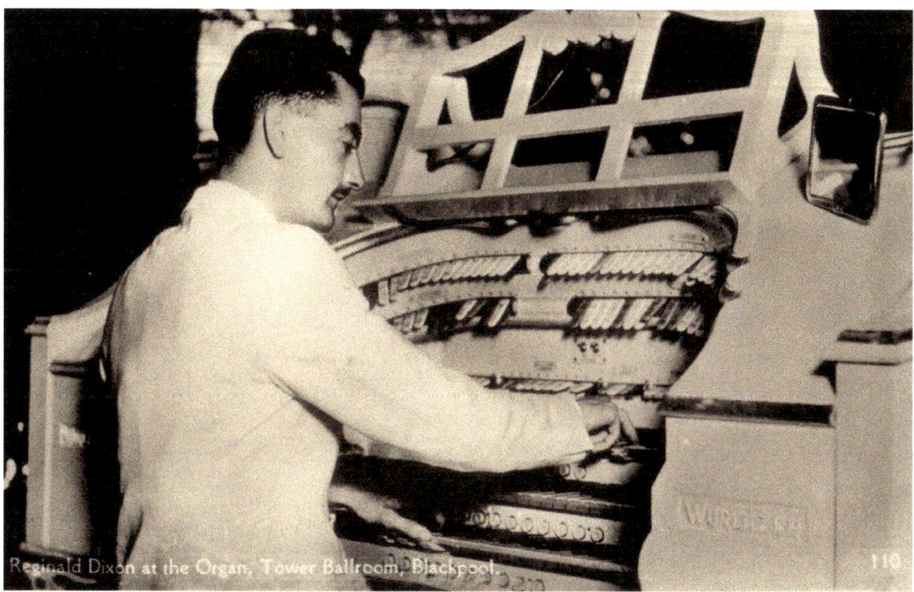

Reginald Dixon at the organ in the Tower Ballroom.

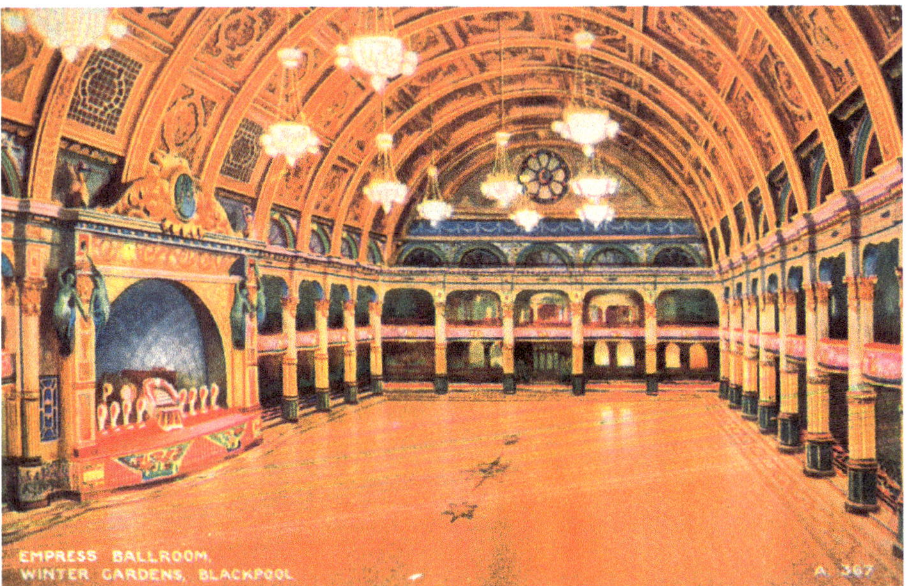



Empress Ballroom, Winter Gardens.

created Empress Building, leading through the Italian Buildings and the giant Ferris wheel.

The Empress Ballroom was one of the largest ballrooms in the world. Having a floor area of 12,500 square feet and a capacity of 3,000, it was hailed as a 'wonder dance floor'. It was well known for hosting annual conferences in the late twentieth century, and in June 2021 celebrated its 125th anniversary.

Not all ballrooms have survived, however. The legendary 3,000-capacity Palace Ballroom opened in July 1904 and was a redesign of the former Alhambra Circus by Frank Matcham. It became part of the ill-fated Palace complex next to the Tower and was demolished in 1961, and mourned by many.

## Winter Gardens and Opera House

In a prominent position in Church Street, in the centre of town, about two minutes' walk from the Promenade and on the original site of Mr Cocker's Bank Hey mansion, stands the Winter Gardens. The concept of 'winter gardens' became popular in English seaside resorts as a venue where people could go in bad weather, as a way of extending the summer season. They were inspired by the splendour of Joseph Paxton's Crystal Palace, built for the Great Exhibition of 1851 in London.

The official opening ceremony on 11 July 1878 was an event of lavish proportions. The mayor (Alderman Cocker) and his committee extended invitations to mayors and mayoresses, together with civic dignitaries, of sixty-eight towns and cities in the country. A new general manager, appointed in 1887,

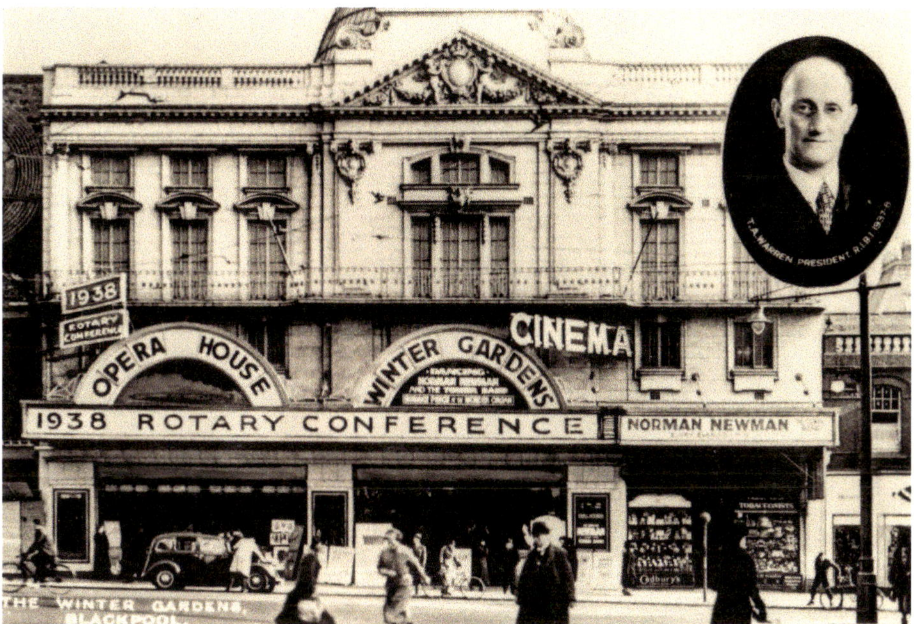


Winter Gardens and Opera House.

had ambitious plans to compete with other attractions in the town. His first summer season's programme of entertainment in 1888 was advertised as offering high-class musical performances and featured a military band and entertainment in the Pavilion comprising of skaters, jugglers, instrumentalists, and vocal duets.

It was said that 'Bill' Holland, dubbed the 'People's Caterer', was employed by the Winter Gardens Company specifically to counter competition from Thomas Sergenson, a successful Blackpool entrepreneur who wanted to start to build his new Grand Theatre in 1888, not far from the Winter Gardens. At the same time William Holland had appointed Frank Matcham to design the 2,500-seat Her Majesty's Opera House, which was completed at a cost of £9,098 and opened on 10 June 1889 with a performance of Gilbert and Sullivan's new opera, *Yeoman of the Guard*. In 1893, electric lighting was installed throughout the entire building at a cost of £3,307.

During the First World War the complex was turned over to the military, and on its reopening was home to many touring shows before being reconstructed in 1938. Opening on 14 June 1939 with a George Formby revue, *Turned Out Nice Again*, the new modernist building became famous for being the first theatre outside London to host the Royal Variety Performance. In 2009, a second one was held. In keeping with the modern age, its speciality was summer spectaculars with top stars of the day and aimed at the holidaymakers. The most recent Royal Variety Performance was held at the Opera House on Sunday 19 November 2020.

After a £4 million refurbishment programme in 1983, the Grade II* listed building was acquired in 2012 by Blackpool Corporation. A brand-new, state-of-the-art,

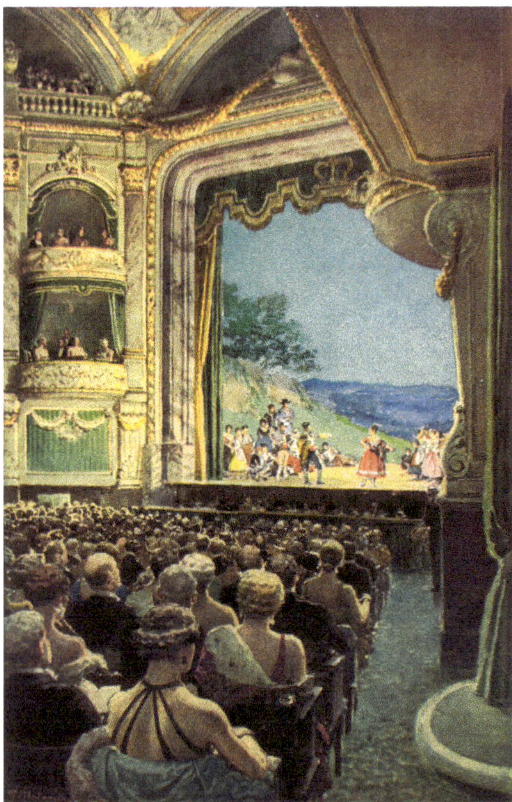

*Left*: Opera House during a performance of Gilbert and Sullivan's *Pirates of Penzance*.

*Below*: Interior of the Winter Gardens.

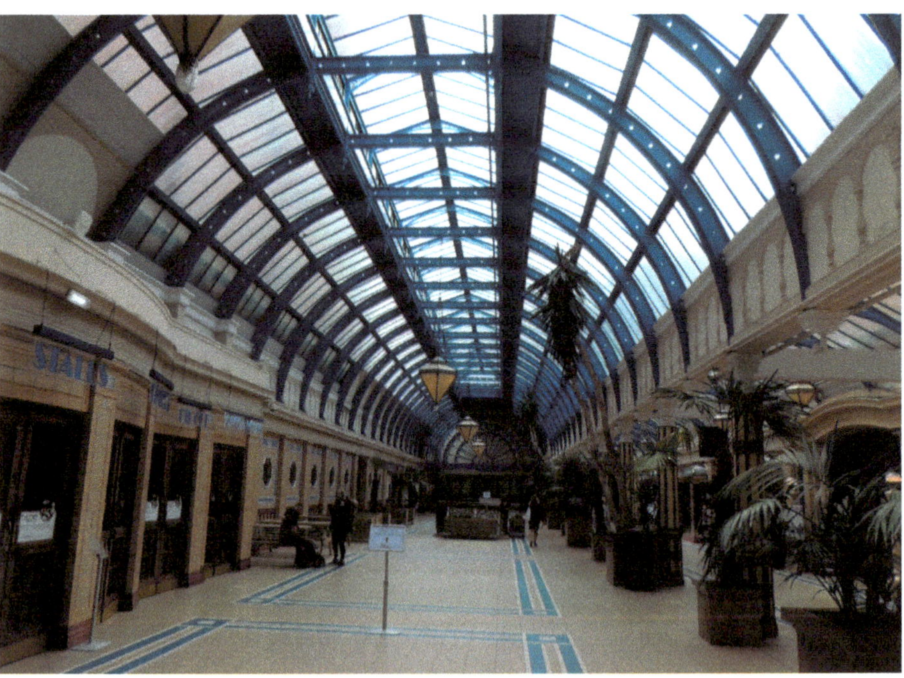

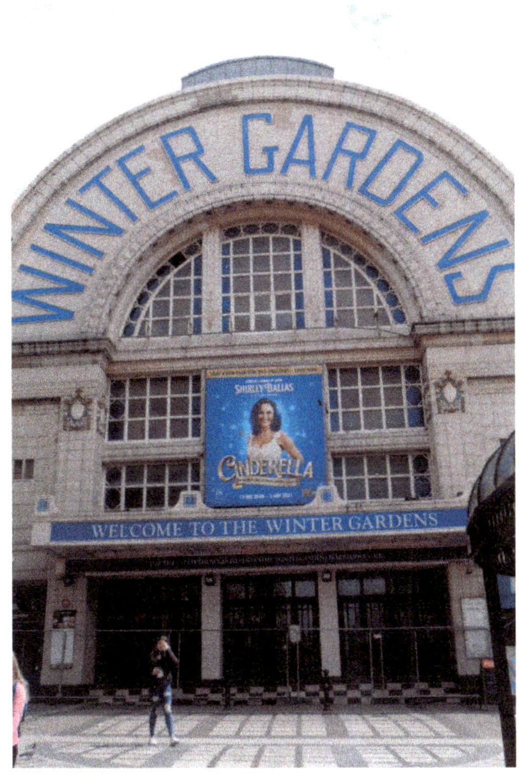

Modern view of the Winter Gardens and Opera House.

£30 million conference and exhibition centre was opened in 2022. The then prime minister, Boris Johnson, unveiled a plaque in the reception hall of the new building on the final day of the Conservative Party Spring Conference, the first time the party has staged a major conference in the resort since 2007.

In 2018, to celebrate 140 years, an exhibition to showcase its illustrious entertainment history was displayed to the public, with posters from past events, programmes, artefacts, and historic photographs. Every year, the world-famous Winter Gardens throws their doors open to the public, allowing them a rare chance to explore this unique entertainment complex.

## Centenarians – Grand Theatre and the Tower

The year 2019 was a landmark one for Blackpool as two special celebrations took place, marking the 125th anniversary of the Tower and the Grand Theatre. More than 350 people attended a special event at the theatre and Sophie, Countess of Wessex, met with some of the key people who have helped to save and restore this iconic building.

The Tower was the first to open, on 14 May 1894. And the dream of the Mayor of Blackpool, John Bickerstaffe, was realised when the opening of this gigantic

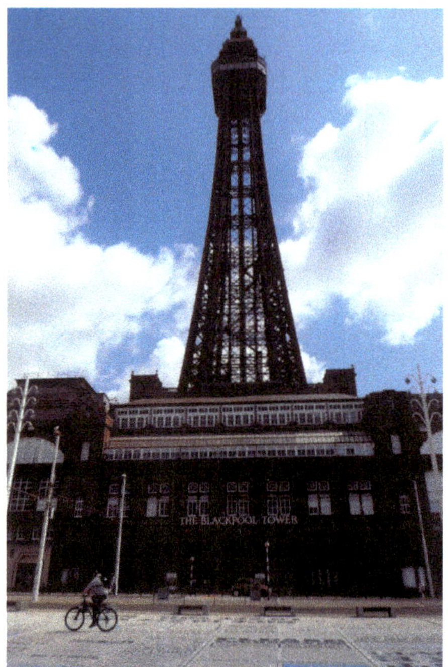

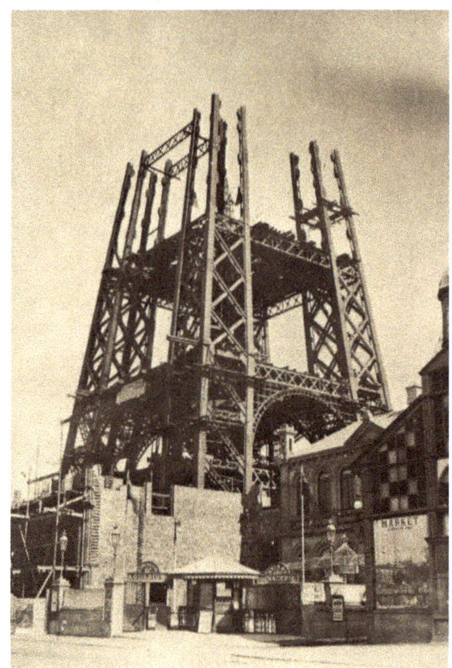

*Above left*: Blackpool Tower and Comedy Carpet.

*Above right*: Blackpool Tower was constructed around an aquarium, 1893.

structure on the Promenade changed the landscape of the town forever. Hailed as a masterpiece of Victorian architecture, visitors clamoured for a chance to ascend to the top of this 518-foot-tall edifice at a rate of over 500 per hour. Crowds were almost fighting to gain admittance to the single elevator that would whisk them to the top to enjoy panoramic views few of them would have witnessed before.

The laying of the foundation stone of the Tower took place in September 1891 and was a day to go down in history as the beginning of the most recognised landmark in the town. From one end of the Promenade to another a brilliant display of bunting served as a backdrop to the spectacle of a procession of over 100 carriages, which stretched two-thirds of a mile in length and was made up of provincial mayors and mayoresses from towns and cities all over England. A line of magistrates and corporate officials set off from the Imperial Hydro Hotel accompanied by twenty-five bands of music, delighting the large crowds lining the magnificently decorated streets. The procession finished at the spot where the stone laying was to be performed by the man of the moment, John Bickerstaffe. He asked Mr Tuke (who, along with fellow architect James Maxwell, had designed the Tower) to present Sir Matthew Ridley Bart White, MP for Blackpool, with a silver trowel on behalf of the directors. Mr Tuke responded by saying, 'Blackpool is well-known throughout England as a famous pleasure resort for the toiling millions.' A gala dinner was held at the Imperial, followed by a grand display of

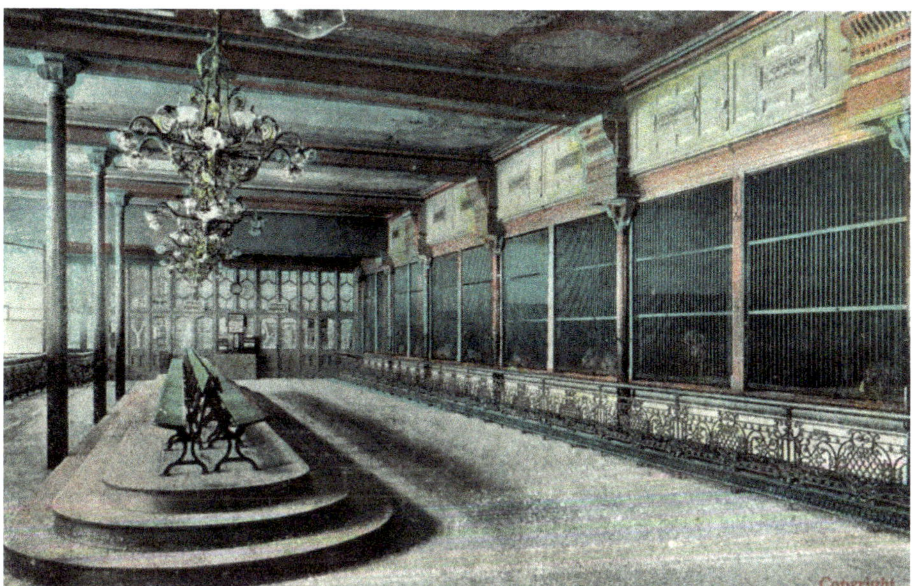

Tower menagerie.

fireworks set off from the North and South piers. Unfortunately, neither Maxwell nor Tuke lived to see the completion of the Tower.

During the construction of the Tower, the aquarium and menagerie (under the ownership of Dr Cocker since 1875) remained open to the public. They were later incorporated into the new Tower building, featuring lions and cheetahs, along with an aviary housing exotic, tropical birds. On the opening day of the Tower, which had no official ceremony to mark the occasion, the visiting public were enthralled by the Blackpool Tower Circus, and over 3,000 visitors attended each performance. The Tower stayed in the ownership of the Bickerstaffe family until 1964, when it was purchased by EMI. After several changes of ownership, the Tower was purchased by Blackpool Council in 2010, and a £20 million investment for the Tower and Promenade included a new entrance, a dungeon created on the site of the old aquarium, and a 4D cinema with a vibrating floor. A new observation platform at the top of the Tower was installed where visitors could experience the thrilling Sky Walk onto the 5-centimetre-thick glass viewing platform, giving a panoramic view of the Irish Sea and beyond.

The Tower was painted silver to celebrate the queen's silver jubilee, and in 1984 when it celebrated its ninetieth birthday a giant inflatable model of King Kong was placed against the building. The Tower is lit up on special occasions, and on its centenary celebrations in 1994 was painted gold by abseiling painters. Recent events have included being illuminated to mark the 75th anniversary of VE day in 2020 and being lit in blue and yellow to express the town's solidarity with the people of Ukraine.

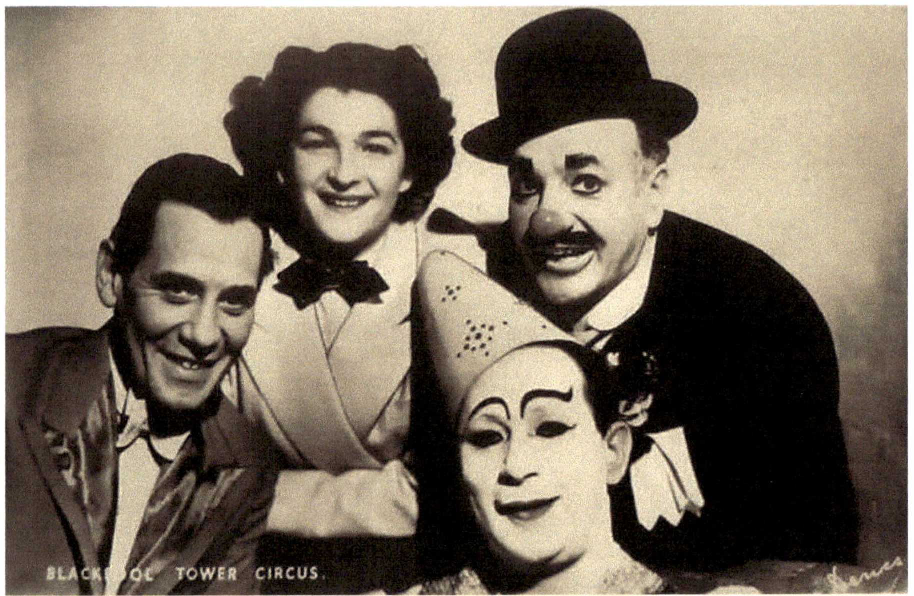



Cast of Blackpool Tower Circus.

Synonymous with the ballroom, the Tower Circus has been delighting audiences to the present day, and has never missed a performance. It is the only surviving permanent circus arena in use and is situated at the base of the Tower, between its four legs. Frank Matcham, whose designs were to transform Blackpool, and are still visible today, redesigned the area in 1900 in a style inspired by Moroccan palaces. An integral part of any circus are the clowns, and between the two world wars Doodles the Clown (alias William McAllister) became the town's most popular circus clown, joining in 1915 and remaining at Blackpool for over twenty years. He was followed by the Italian-born Charlie Cairolli, who made his first appearance in 1939 and, like Reginald Dixon, entertained audiences for over forty years. Charlie came from a family of established circus performers and made regular appearances on television and in Royal Variety Performances and pantomimes. Instantly recognisable with his red nose and Chaplin-style bowler hat, he had the distinction of performing thirty-two consecutive seasons at Blackpool. He retired in 1979 due to ill health, to be succeeded by his son, Charlie Jr, for several years.

Charlie Cairolli Sr died a year after his retirement on 17 February 1980 at the age of seventy. In 2000, he was awarded a posthumous Lifetime Award from the *World's Fair Circus* newspaper, which was presented to his widow, Violetta. As a tribute to his outstanding contribution to the resort a statue of him stands in the Tower. In October 2018, he also had the honour of his own heritage tram boat – Car 227, nicknamed 'Charlie's Tram' – which had been restored by the Civic Trust to its 1934 condition, painted in red and ivory livery, and decorated with an image of Charlie himself.

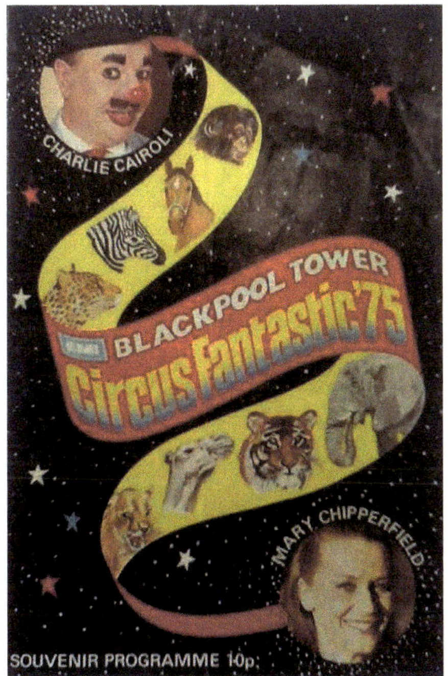


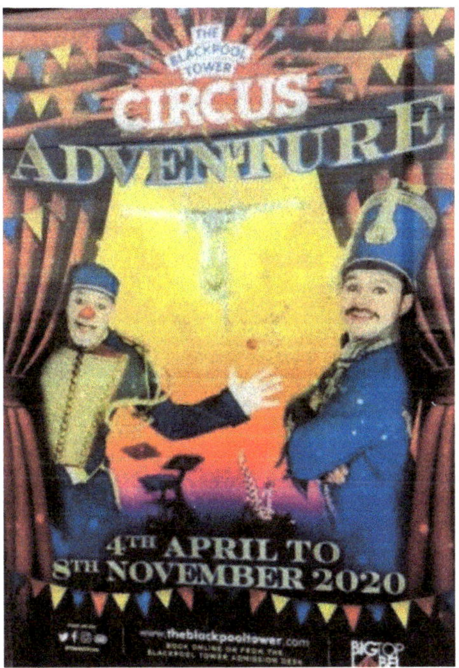


*Above left*: Souvenir programme for Circus Fantastic, 1975.

*Above right*: Tower Circus, 2020.

Talented clowns still appear at the Tower Circus. Although the Cairolli name is no longer here, its place has been filled from 1991 with the Endresz circus family. Originally from Hungary, they have established themselves as legends in their own right. Laci Endresz Jr, the son of the director of the Tower Circus, performs as Mooky the Clown having first appeared on stage at the age of four.

## The Grand Theatre

Two months after the opening of the Tower in 1994, residents and visitors alike flocked to the opening night at the Grand Theatre to see a production of *Hamlet*, starring the renowned actor Wilson Barrett. A commemorative programme was printed on pure silk and perfumed with 'Tower Bouquet'. The theatre took just nine months to build and cost £20,000. It was the brainchild of Blackpool's first successful theatre manager, Mr Thomas Sergenson, who secured the services of Frank Matcham. It was unique in that it was the first theatre in Blackpool to be totally electric and to have a fully cantilevered circle, which eliminated the need for pillars and gave every seat a clear view. Mr Matcham also invented crash doors, enabling a quick evacuation of the building if necessary.

The theatre is still known as Matcham's masterpiece. The press who attended the opening said, 'Mr Matcham must be heartily congratulated on having designed a building worthy of being classed among the leading theatres of the country.' Thomas Sergenson's career flourished as the theatre attracted names like Sarah Bernhardt, Lily Langtree, Ellen Terry and Dan Leno. His tenure lasted until 1909, when the theatre was sold to the Blackpool Tower Company for £47,000. In the 1930s, the top performer was the singer-comedian Gracie Fields, who appeared at the Grand twice nightly for the summer season from 1932 to 1938, supported by a 'bumper holiday cast'.

Summer seasons at the Grand showcased the cream of comedy for holidaymakers to enjoy, with top names like Arthur Askey and Hylda Baker. It remained open during the Second World War, presenting West End successes such

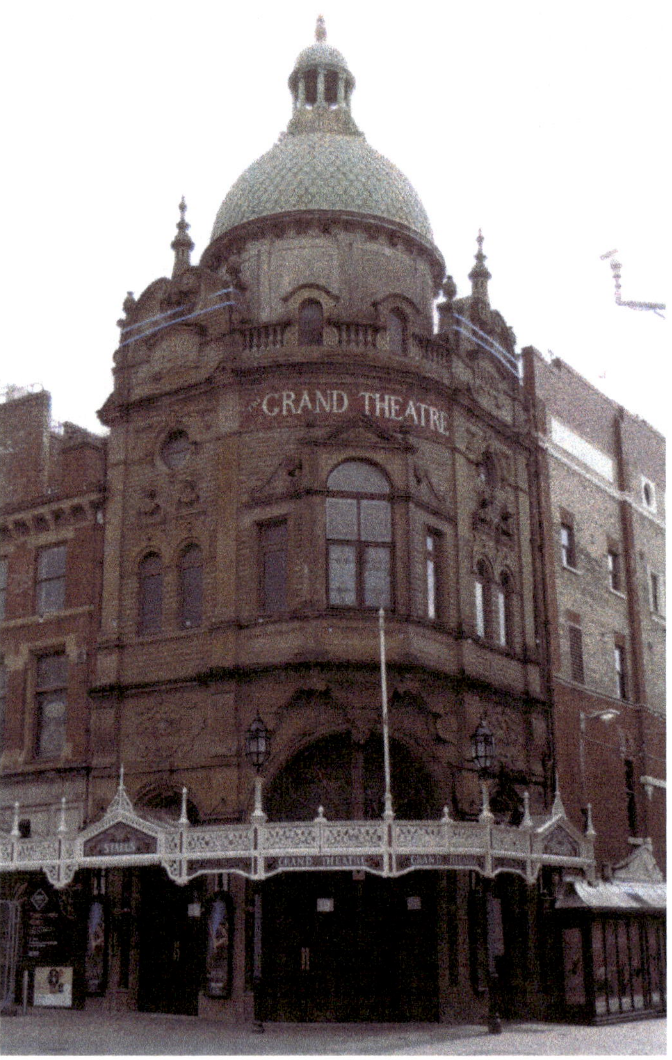

Grand Theatre.

as Noel Coward's *Blithe Spirit* and *This Happy Breed*. The magic of Blackpool in the 1950s was recreated in November 2017 when 1950s pop idol Marty Wilde, as part of his Solid Gold Rock and Roll Tour, performed at the Grand with Mike Berry, Eden Kaine and Mark Wynter. The 1960s saw the regular appearance of comedy stars such as Sid James and Freddie Frinton.

In the 1970s, however, the theatre suffered a period of decline and faced possible closure. Although it had been awarded Grade II* status in 1971, there was talk of demolition to make way for a new store. Through the determined efforts of a voluntary organisation – Friends of the Grand, which had been formed in 1973 and had amongst its members, Violet Carson, Ken Dodd, Timothy West and Prunella Scales – the theatre was saved. The group's most famous founder member, Ken Dodd, made his first appearance on 29 March 1978 to help raise funds. Over forty years later more than 1,700 members continue to support the theatre.

After a brief spell as a bingo hall, the Grand reopened as a theatre on 23 March 1981, having been bought by the Grand Theatre Trust in 1980 and being restored to its original condition. The opening production was the Old Vic Tour of *a Merchant of Venice*, starring Timothy West and Prunella Scales. A Royal Gala Performance was held on 29 May in the presence of the then Prince Charles with a star-studded bill, including Petula Clark, Violet Carson, Jimmy Jewel and Barbara Windsor.

A five-year programme commenced in 1988 to restore the theatre back to its nineteenth-century footprint. In 2001, the Glorious Grand Appeal was launched, and the following year a gala celebration was held with a performance of *Mikado* by the Carl Rosa Opera Company. The year 2019 marked the official 125th birthday of the opening of this iconic theatre.

Fundraising continues to be the main objective to help preserve the Grand for future generations.

## Comedy

On the seafront, just in front of the Tower, is a celebration of the resort's long association with comedy. This unique artwork, commissioned by Blackpool Council and four years in the making, is the Comedy Carpet. It features names, jokes, songs, and comedy catchphrases of over a thousand of the best-known comedians and comic entertainers, of which around 80 per cent had appeared in the resort. Who better to perform the grand opening ceremony on 10 October 2011 than the 'master of mirth' Sir Ken Dodd, whose long association with entertainment in Blackpool spanned over sixty years and included a total of 2,000 appearances. Starring in six summer seasons at the Opera House, he performed his last headline season in *Laughter Spectacular 81*, for which he was rewarded with a place on the Opera House roll of honour, displayed in the Church Street entrance of the Winter Gardens.

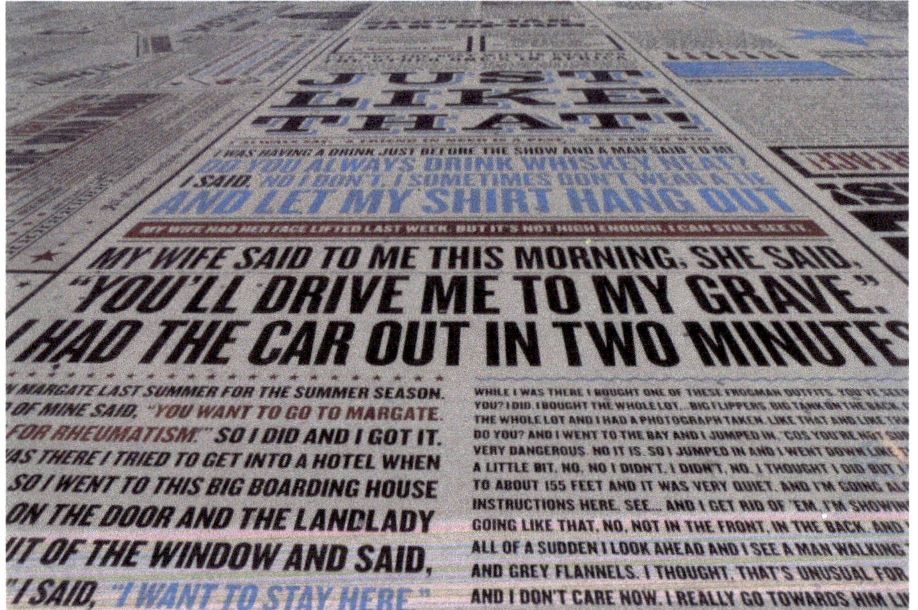

Comedy Carpet.

When two promising young comedians called Eric Bartholomew and Ernest Wiseman appeared at the Old Palace Theatre, Blackpool, in 1940, little did they know that when they reappeared as a double act nearly ten years later at the Old Feldman's Theatre in April 1949, it would be the start of an association with the resort that was to last for many years. The *Blackpool Gazette* reported: 'Morecambe and Wise, a couple of young funsters have a promising style and a good comedy line.' They went on to perform in the town more than 1,000 times, appearing in seven theatres, six summer seasons and at the top of the bill for the 1955 Royal Variety Performance at the Winter Gardens. The pair was particularly remembered for their classic white suits and top hats, worn in the highest-rated Christmas special in 1977. To celebrate their 50th anniversary, Madame Tussauds in Blackpool restyled their wax, white-suited figures, entitled 'Still bringing us sunshine fifty years on'. To mark the 75th anniversary of their debut performance as a double act, an 8-foot, bronzed sculpture was unveiled at the Winter Gardens on 14 October 2016.

The 1930s were a golden era of Blackpool as a traditional entertainment centre, and attracted global stars. In 1932, the town played host to the world's number-one comedy team, Laurel and Hardy, when they visited the town on a promotional tour, staying at the Metropole Hotel. In 1947, when topping a variety bill at the Old Palace Theatre, they were given an ecstatic welcome by the crowds who mobbed them wherever they went. Ollie was said to have remarked, 'We were lucky to leave the town in one piece.'

The legendary George Formby, famous for his song *A Little Bit of Blackpool Rock*, appeared many times in Blackpool, and as a testament to his popularity

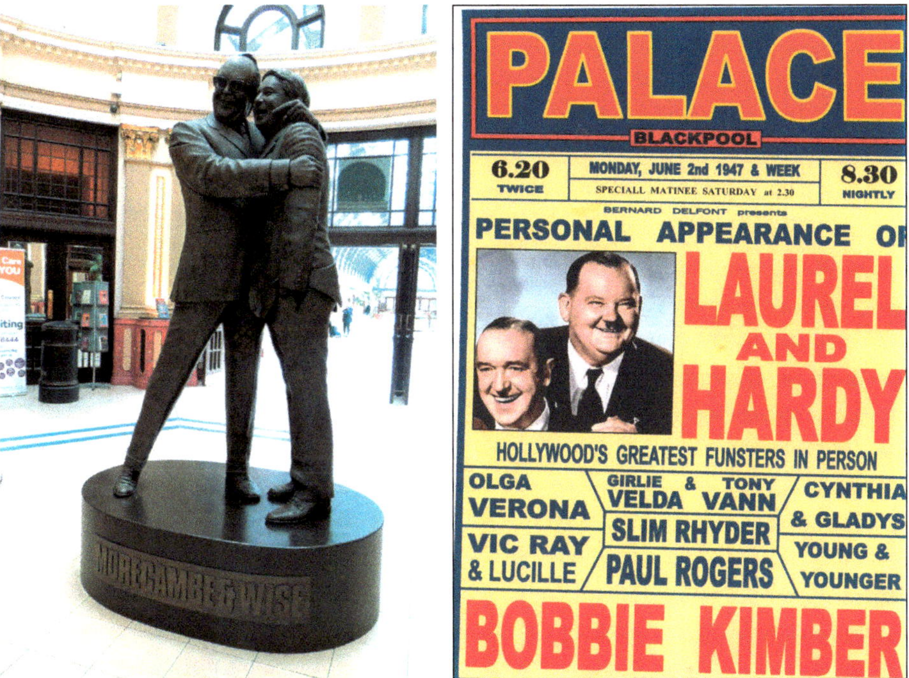


*Above left*: Morecambe and Wise statue in Winter Gardens.

*Above right*: Poster of Laurel and Hardy at the Palace.

the George Formby Society still holds its quarterly conventions at the Imperial Hotel. One of Britain's most popular present-day comedians is Bolton-born Peter Kay. In 2000, he staged the show *Live at the Top of the Tower* and in 2009 hosted the Royal Variety Performance at the Opera House – the first time it had been presented in the town since 1955. Blackpool is still at the forefront of comedy, and making the Fylde Coast laugh since 2002 is the Comedy Station Comedy Club opposite the Tower on Bank Hey Street.

## Walking on the Water – the Town with Three Piers

For many, the seaside pier is perhaps the most iconic symbol of the British seaside holiday. On 16 May 1863 there was a promise of a 'grand day out' in Blackpool when the newspapers advertised special cheap excursion trains from Lancashire's main towns to attend the opening of the resort's first pier. The *Preston Chronicle* of 23 May reported, 'The rejoicings were such as will be remembered, for never since Blackpool obtained a place on the map of Lancashire was there such a festive demonstration within the range of its health inspiring breezes.'

Streamers, flags, and banners decorated the streets. The pier was adorned with bunting and, at 11 a.m., the day commenced with a procession through the town. Headed by the 19th Manchester Lancashire Artillery Corps, deputations of Freemen and Oddfellows were joined by representatives of the various trades of the town, such as butchers, joiners, and shrimpers. Behind the Ancient Order of Druids were two men staggering under a huge banner representing joiners and mechanics, and at the rear were the donkey boys and chimney sweep. At various stages a couple of bathing vans struggled to keep up with the party. The procession ended at 2 p.m. in the Square, opposite the Clifton Arms.

Between 1864 and 1867, a landing jetty was built on the pier head to enable passengers to embark and disembark the steamers that offered pleasure trips to surrounding areas. Unfortunately, seaside piers have always been prone to fires, and there have been several over the years. The most serious was the 1921 destruction of the beautiful Indian Pavilion, which had been built in 1874 and was extensively used for concert performances, with a full orchestra and an entrance fee of 1s. History repeated itself when the new Pavilion was destroyed by fire in 1938 and replaced the following year by the art deco Pavilion Theatre.

It was described as the finest marine pier in the country, offering high-class entertainment of bands and orchestral music, with its own orchestra (pictured here). Many guest artists from abroad, such as the Royal Roumanian Sextet, performed on the pier from the Edwardian period right up to the Second World War. It changed its name to the North Pier Theatre and from 1924 to 1956 the famous production *On With The Show* was presented, starring Frankie Vaughan, Frank Randle, Albert Modley and Tessie O'Shea. This was replaced in 1957 by a

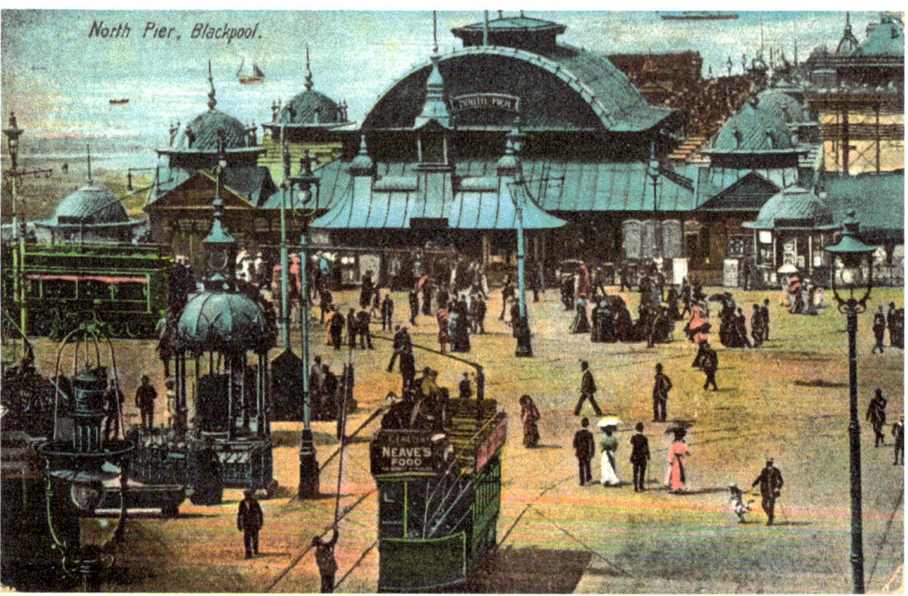


North Pier.

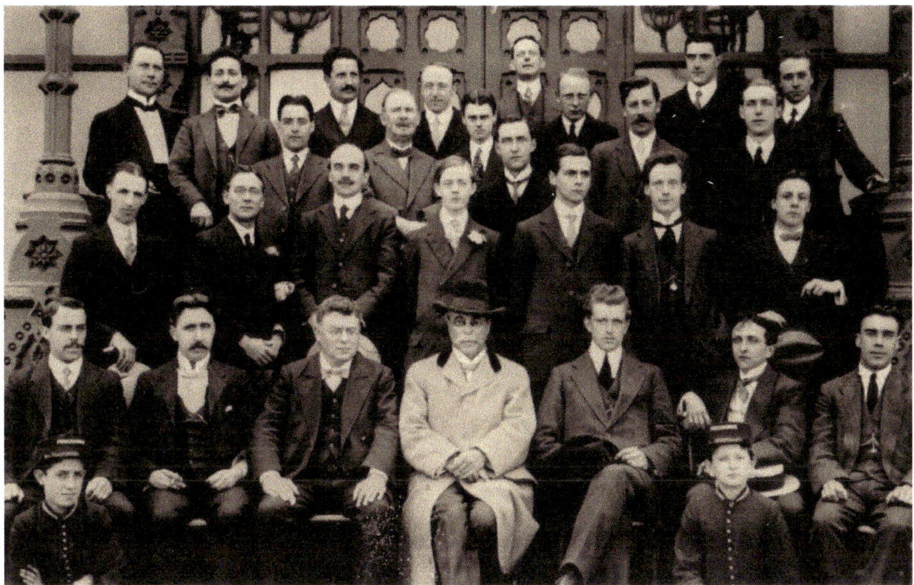

North Pier Orchestra.

popular entertainment show called *Bernard Delfont Presents Show of Stars,* which ran until 1982, attracting such well-known stars of the day as Bruce Forsyth, Morecambe and Wise, Teddy Johnson and Pearl Carr, as well as the puppets Pinky and Perky. The historic North Pier Theatre has recently been renamed the Joe Longthorne Theatre, to commemorate the late entertainer who was honoured for his thirty years of entertainment in Blackpool.

Piers now have to adapt to changing tastes, and on the North Pier the old solarium has been transformed into a lounge and conservatory bar.

After the success of the North Pier, it was decided to build another to the south of the Promenade. Called the South Jetty, it was opened on 30 May 1868, but this time there was no grand ceremony to mark the occasion. The pier did not prove popular at first, but all this changed when Robert Bickerstaffe was appointed manager. He introduced steamboat excursions and arranged for a band to play when the trippers returned for open-air dancing.

The short-lived Electric Grotto Railway built by Messrs Meinhardt in 1904 only lasted until 1907, but roller skating on Central Pier lasted for forty years, from 1909 to 1949.

Offering affordable entertainment to the masses, in contrast to the more upmarket North Pier, the new pier was dubbed the 'People's Pier', as, in addition to open-air dancing, it offered roller skating, which could be enjoyed by the whole family. To celebrate the 150th anniversary of the opening, in March 2018 a day of entertainment was held consisting of magic shows, treasure hunts, and live music. It was attended by the Mayor of Blackpool.

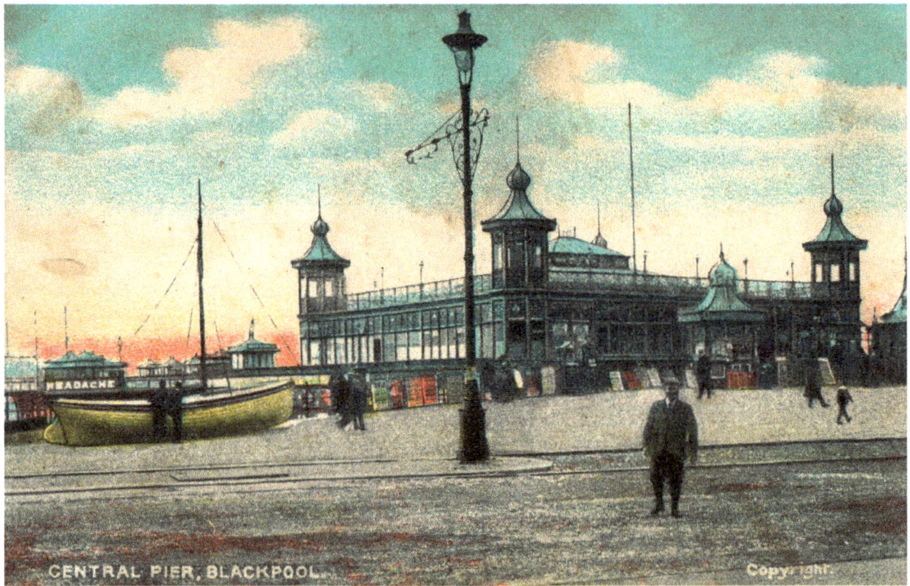

Central Pier.

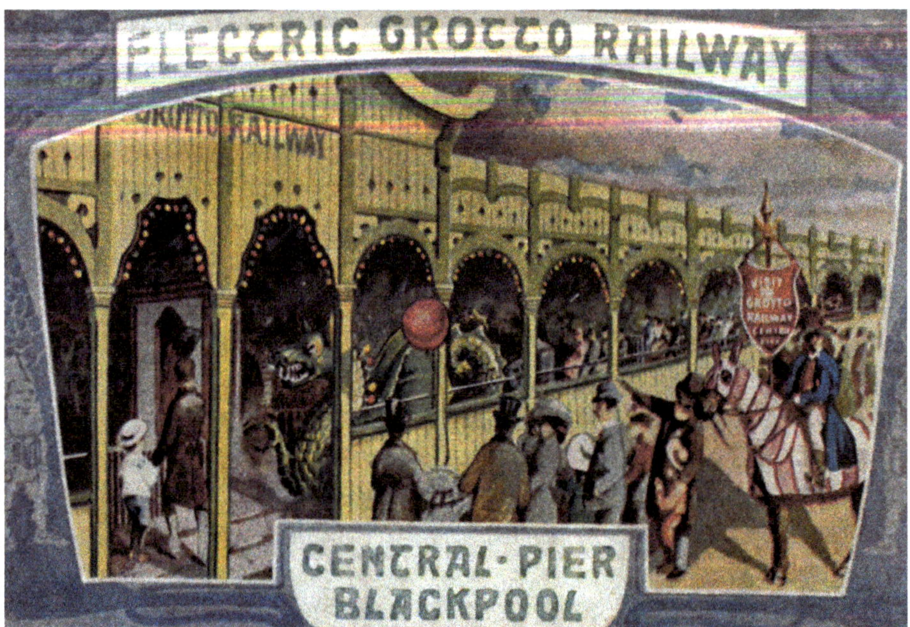



Electric Grotto Railway.

In 1967, the Dixieland Palace replaced the Central Pier Pavilion above the Golden Goose arcade. On 22 September it was destroyed by fire but was quickly reopened. A giant 108-foot Ferris wheel was erected in 1990, sixty-two years after the dismantling of the big wheel at the Winter Gardens. To enhance the visitor experience for the future, a brand-new, even bigger wheel is being built as part of a £4 million upgrade.

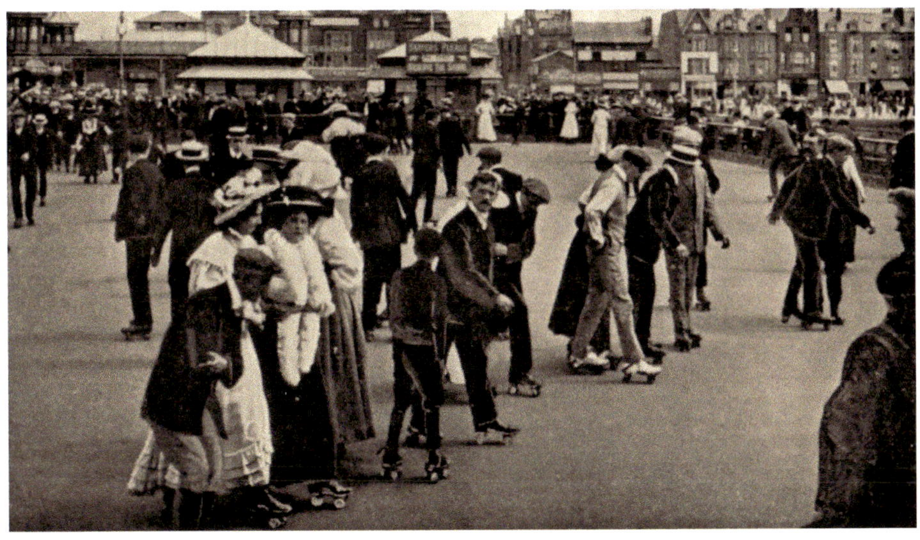

Roller skating on Central Pier.

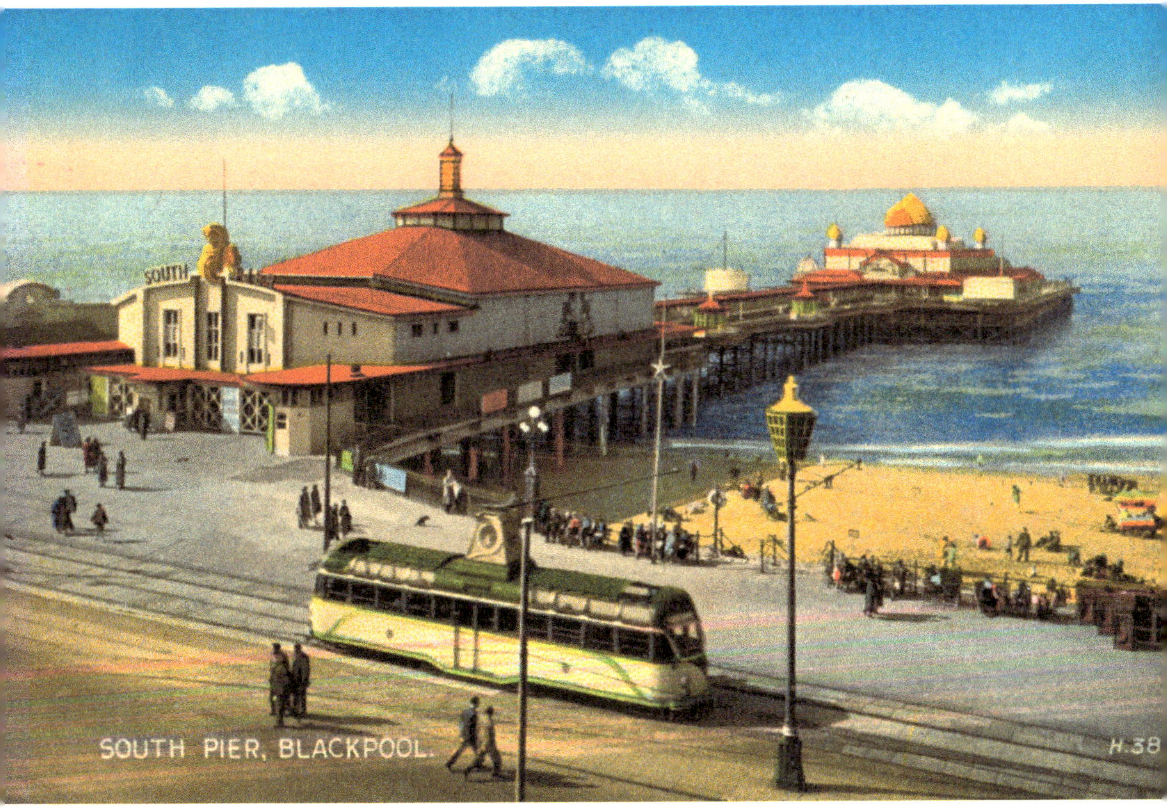

South Pier.

The third pier to be made in Blackpool was constructed at a cost of £50,000 and opened on Good Friday 1893 with a choir, two brass bands, and an orchestra. The shortest of the three piers, at 163 yards long, it was named Victoria Pier and was considered more upmarket than the North and Central piers. The 3,000-capacity Grand Pavilion was opened on 20 May. In 1930, it was renamed South Pier.

## Golden Mile of Fun

It was announced in the press in 2011 that Blackpool's Golden Mile, the stretch between the North and South piers, was set for a makeover and a name change. Blackpool Council suggested the name Queen Elizabeth Promenade in the hope that it would change its somewhat tarnished reputation of the last few years. However, to most people it is still looked on fondly as the Golden Mile, as it has been since its conception around 1897, when it offered amusements galore. That year, the corporation banned from the beach all unlicensed traders, who simply moved their stalls to the private gardens of the houses across from the Promenade and set up business again. These makeshift stalls started off with fortune tellers, palmists, phrenologists, and quack doctors, many operating from primitive huts and tents.

By 1929 the Golden Mile stretched from the southern end of Coney Island to Toyland at the north. In the 1930s it gained a reputation as staging lurid and notorious sideshows. The curious visitors rolled up to see 'the biggest rat in the world'; Charlie Dunlop, the India Rubber Man; the Bearded Lady, the ugliest woman in the world (you could get £1,000 for marrying her, it was claimed!); 'Ubangi Savages'; and the Living Hands of Patna, a woman with half a body.

King of the sideshows was a Burnley-born showman by the name of Luke Gannon. Visitors were soon parting from their hard-earned cash to see exhibits of starving brides allegedly living in a glass case for twenty-eight days. Fascinated onlookers gasped as a lady had to live in a large barrel, surviving ten days without food or water. When she suddenly decided to quit on day nine, an angry mob ensued and the barrel was rolled across the Promenade and onto the beach, to the delight of the crowd. Mr Gannon's most notorious crowd puller was Harold Davidson, a rector of Stiffkey, Norfolk, who had been defrocked for alleged immorality, which he strenuously denied. This was to be Gannon's greatest money spinner as the reverend gentleman was also exhibited in a barrel, where he was to starve for fourteen days. Huge crowds queued for the privilege of peering at him through a window. It attracted such great numbers that the police were called, and Gannon and Davidson were charged with obstruction. Despite attempts by the council to stop the showman's attraction, Luke Gannon continued to exhibit his protégé, but his fame soon diminished. Davidson came to a sticky end when, while giving a sermon in a lion's cage in Skegness, he made the mistake of treading on a lion's tail and was viciously attacked, dying two days later on 6 October 1939.

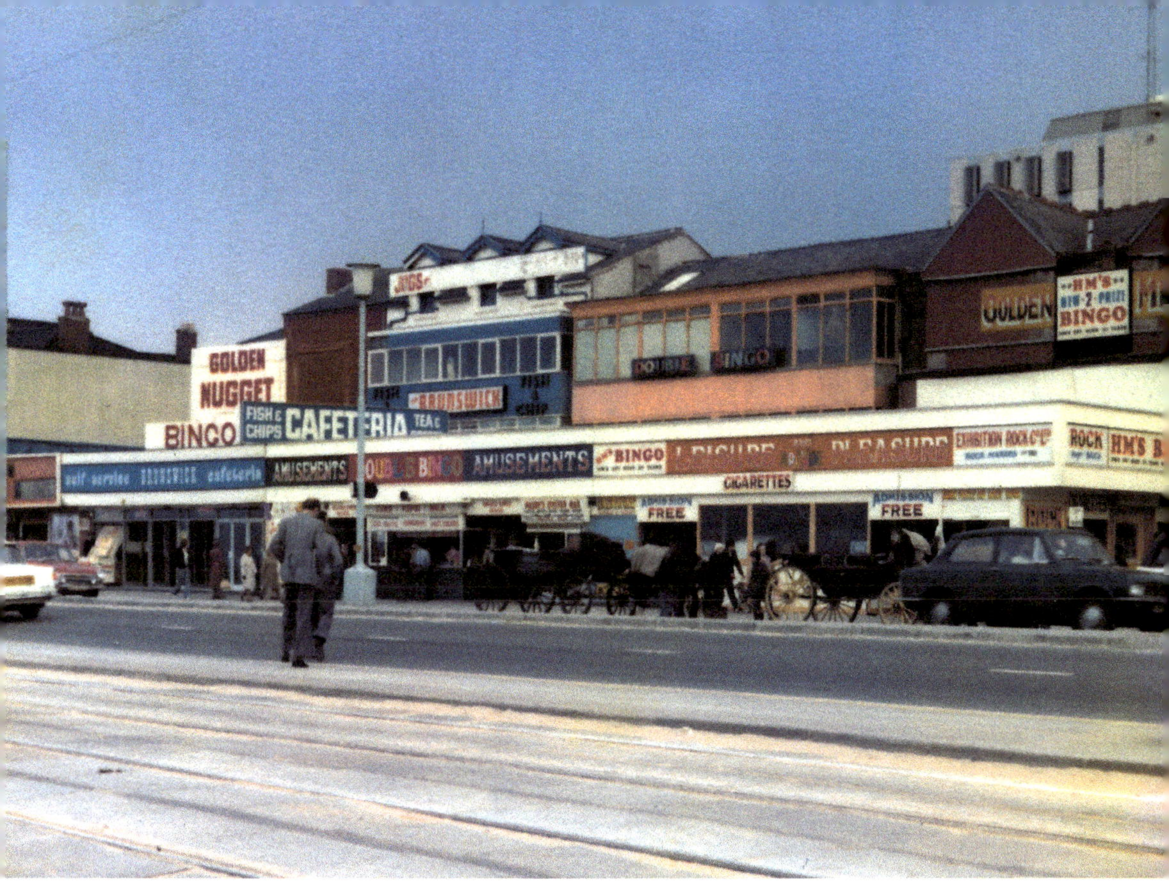

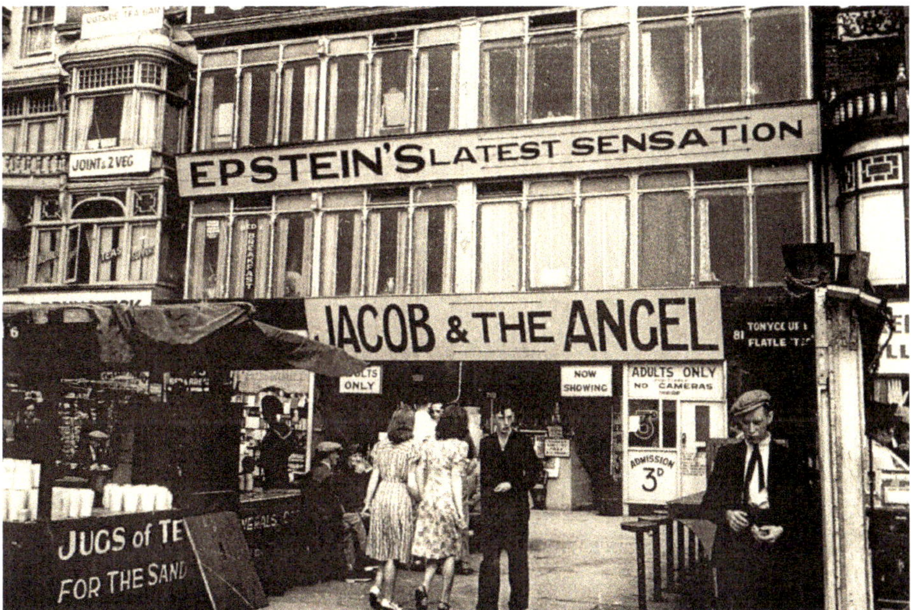

Golden Mile.



Golden Mile sideshow, 1942.

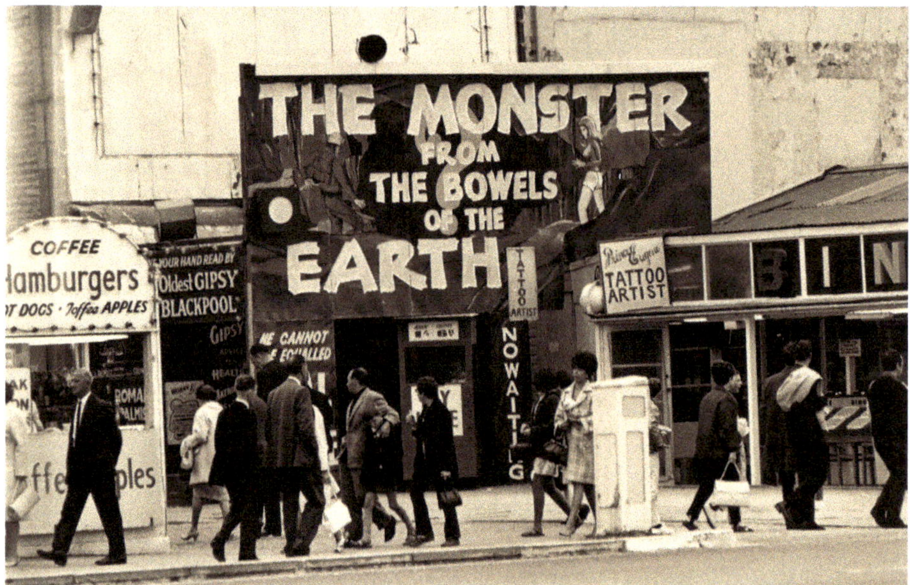


Tacky Blackpool.

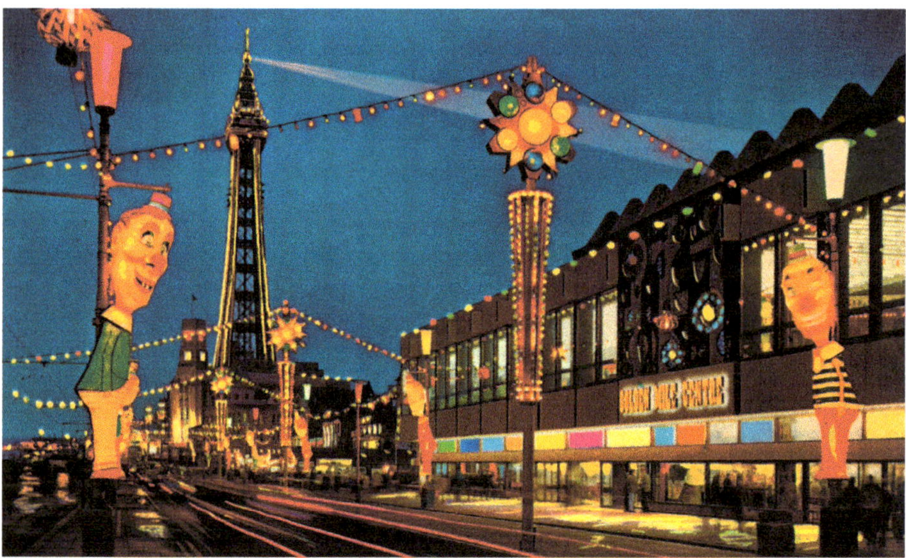

Illuminations along the Golden Mile.

Probably the most infamous showman on the Golden Mile, he was cremated at Carleton Cemetery.

In the mid-1950s the Golden Mile was again under scrutiny when it was accused in the press of harbouring degrading sex shows. However, it was also advertised as 'the most amazing seaside show on earth' and described as the dearest entertainment in the world – 'when the public pay and showmen collect'.

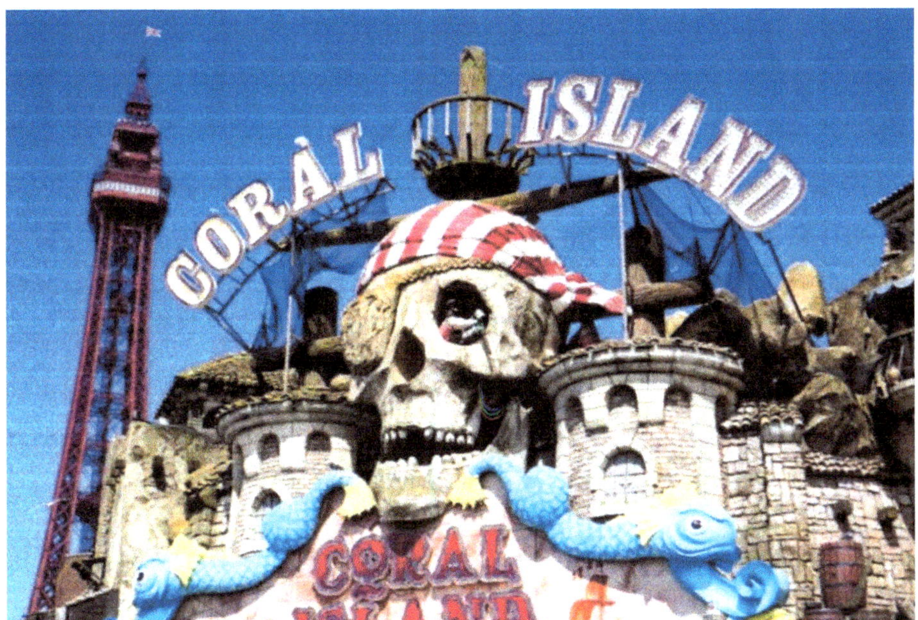


Coral Island.

Now the entertainments on the Golden Mile are mostly indoors, including several family attractions and amusement arcades, Coral Island, Funland and Oasis, and the famous Madame Tussaud's waxworks. To keep pace with modern times, a new entertainment centre is planned to attract new audiences to the venue on the Promenade, as part of a £2.3 million investment.

## Pleasure Beach – from Switchbacks to White-knuckle Rides

The end of the Victorian age heralded a period of great enterprise in the development of Blackpool. A shrewd businessman called William George Bean was to build a place of entertainment that would put the town firmly on the map. The southern part of the Promenade was largely undeveloped and was occupied by a gypsy encampment. Visiting Coney Island in America, William Bean was inspired by the spectacular rides there. This marked the beginning of imported rides from USA, such as the single switchback railway on the sands, operated by John Outhwaite. The switchback was soon followed by the American Carousel and the Hotchkiss Bicycle Railroad ride, which had a grooved monorail, over which bicycles were hung. A partnership was formed between Bean and Outhwaite, and the Pleasure Beach was born.

In 1904, a thrilling ride called Sir Hiram Maxim's Flying Machine arrived. Although it has since been modified, it is the oldest amusement park ride in

Europe and the only example of its type in the world. As it was being erected on the Pleasure Beach prior to its opening in August of that year, the man himself, Sir Maxim, visited the town and invited the Mayor of Blackpool and members of the corporation to a celebratory luncheon at the Hotel Metropole.

The scenic railway was invented by an American, LaMarcus A. Thompson – widely regarded as the father of the American roller coaster – and operated from 1907 to 1933. The Velvet Coaster, designed by William Homer Strickler, so-called because of its open carriages lined with velvet seats, was followed by the Lighthouse Helter Skelter and the River Caves of the World, both imported from America. A record 3 million people visited the Pleasure Beach

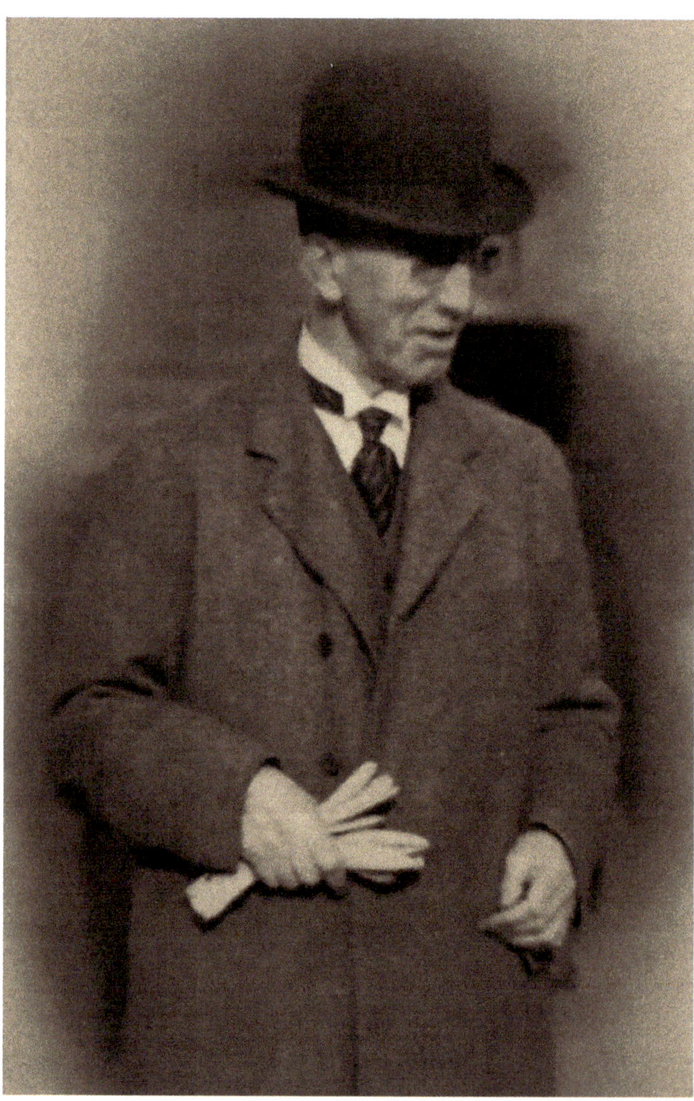

William George Bean.

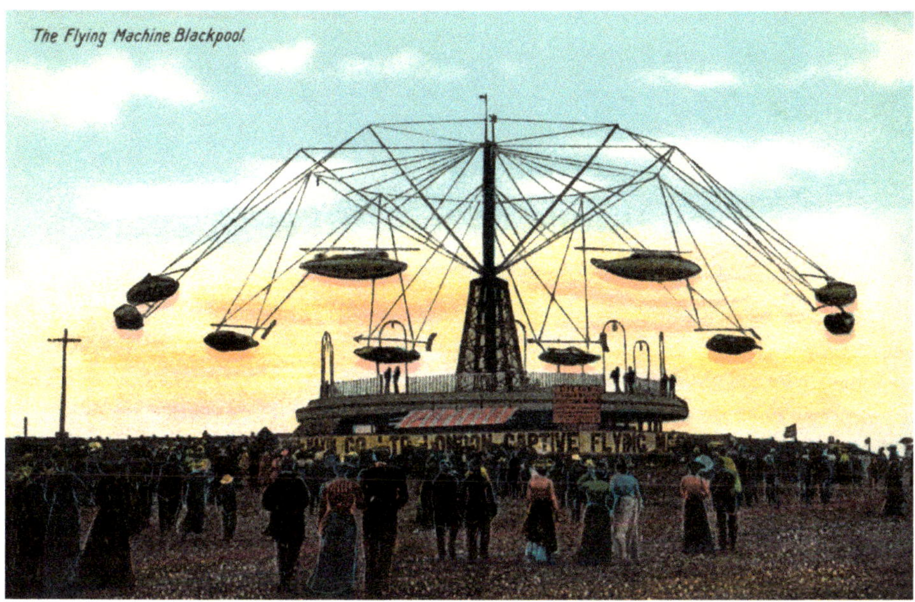


Flying Machine on Pleasure Beach.

in 1906 as the public clamoured for the spills and thrills of these amazing new rides.

John Outhwaite died in 1911, leaving W. G. Bean to operate alone. The gypsy encampment was dismantled and the gypsies evicted, allowing the construction of new rides and novelties each season. The next major development was the casino at the Pleasure Beach entrance, completed in 1913 and designed by local architect R. B. Mather. Built in the style of an Indian Palace and illuminated at night, it had an East Asian-themed tearoom, restaurant, grill room, billiard room, and shop. It also offered dancing in the afternoon.

This iconic ride, which opened in Easter 1922, proved very popular with its dark tunnels, passageways and pressure places, which when walked on let out animal noises. It was the brainchild of William Homer Strickler, born in Philadelphia, USA, in 1845 and arriving in Blackpool in the 1920s with grand plans to build amusement rides. It was a walk-through dark ride and comprised a large wooden boat mounted on a rocking mechanism. It was rebuilt in 1935 to the same design, but subsequently altered. Out of use since 2008, it now functions as an architectural feature, forming the final entrance portal for visitors to the Pleasure Beach. In 2017, it was awarded Grade II listed status, being the oldest surviving example of the ride in the world. The same year Mr Strickler also introduced the Virginia Reel, which stood for sixty years. A year later came the classic wooden roller coaster, the Big Dipper. It was built at a cost of £25,000 and is also Grade II listed. The second oldest roller coaster in use in Britain, and is one of only thirty-seven Second World War wooden roller coasters worldwide (of which four are at the Pleasure Beach). Sadly, William Strickler died after a fall while building Noah's

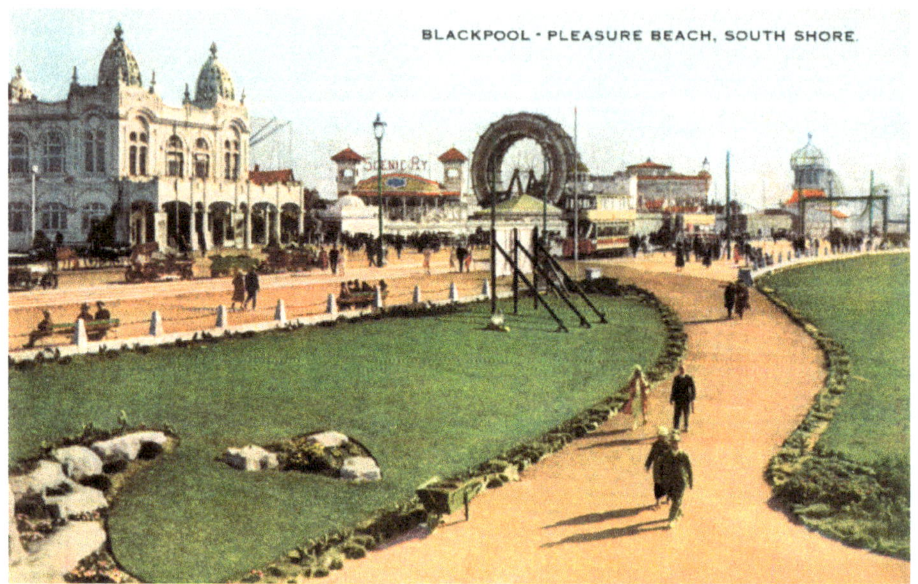


Entrance to Pleasure Beach.

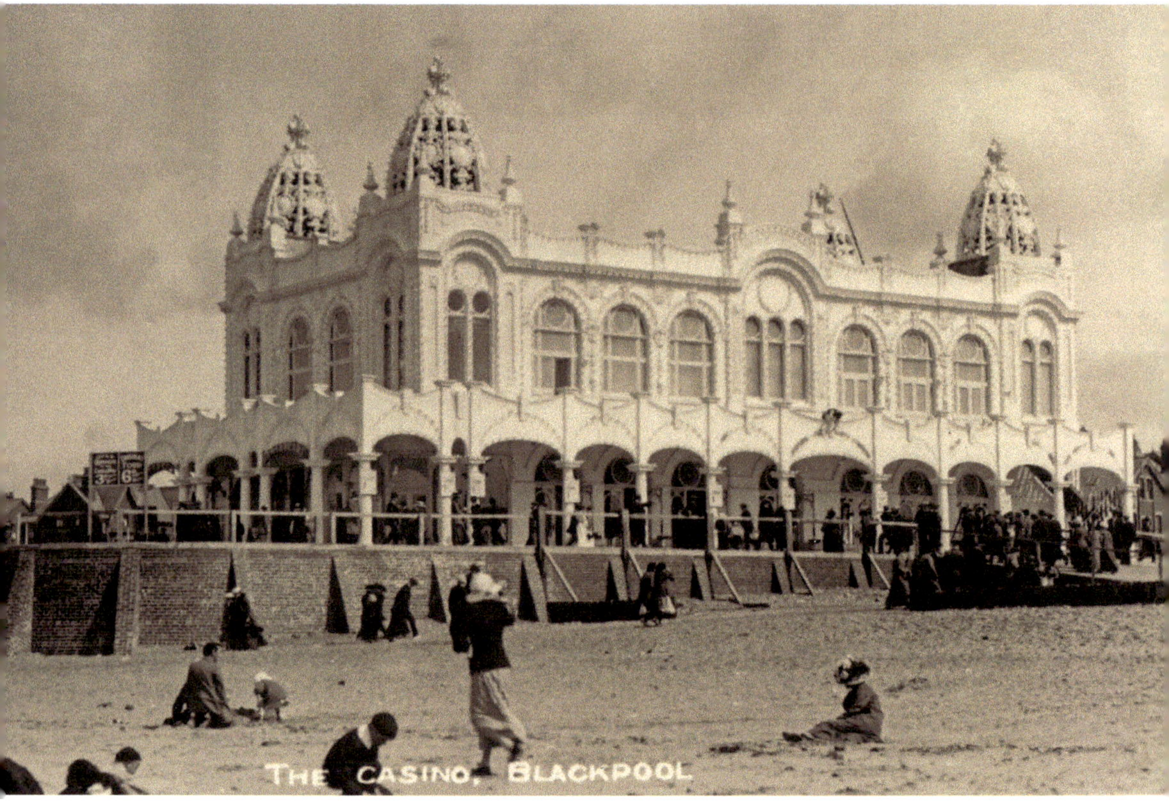

The Casino, Pleasure Beach.

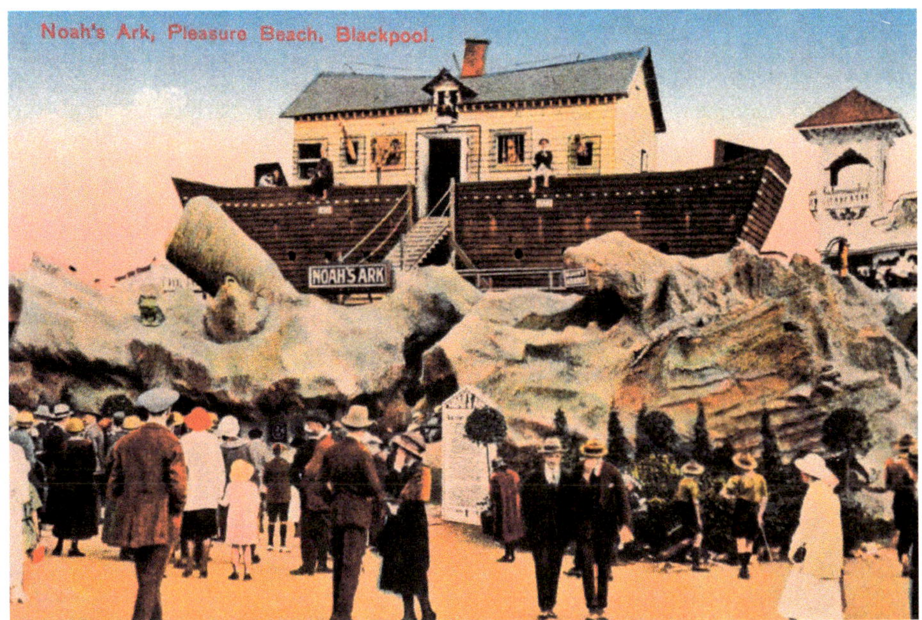


Noah's Ark, Pleasure Beach.

Ark in Southport in 1930, and is buried in Layton Cemetery, close by the William Bean Memorial and the Thompson family grave.

When William George Bean died in 1929, he had also been a respected alderman. He was listed with others in the borough in a report dated 7 January 1933 as 'giants of their time who pointed Blackpool in the right direction'. The management of the park passed to his son-in-law, Leonard Thompson, who together with his wife, Doris (Bean's daughter), continued to introduce new rides. In the 1930s, the Fun House, which replaced the earlier House of Nonsense, was immensely popular until 1991, when it suffered a devastating fire, an event reported in the press as 'The Day the Fun died'. All that was saved was the head of the famous laughing clown, a symbol of Blackpool for sixty years, which was later restored. The ghost train, which opened in 1930, was designed by Joseph Emberton and it is significant for being the first real ghost train in the world, based on the name of a popular play at the time.

The Grand National, another attraction awarded Grade II listing in 2017, was a wooden roller coaster of 1935, completely replaced in 1990 with the original design. It is only the fifth example in the world of a Möbius Loop roller coaster, of which only two pre-war examples survive.

In July 1937, a new 2,000-seat ice drome was built – the world's first purpose-built ice rink (as reported in the Guinness Book of Records). It had public skating, was a venue for ice dance clubs and hosted an annual ice show. It is still in use and is the home of the world-famous Hot Ice Show. The casino was also rebuilt to an art deco design by Joseph Emberton, complete with grill room, American soda bar, and a banqueting hall for 700 diners.

## Roller Coaster Ride to Success

When Leonard Thompson died in 1976, his son Geoffrey became managing director of the park, and his widow Doris was appointed chairman. Many new rides came into operation, including the Revolution, the first 360-degree roller coaster in Europe; the Avalanche, the UK's only bobsleigh ride; and the Big One, which at the time was the tallest, fastest roller coaster ride in the world. Doris Thompson was a director of the Pleasure Beach for more than sixty years, celebrating her 100th birthday still testing all the new white-knuckle rides. She died at the age of 101, on 23 June 2004, less than two weeks after her son Geoffrey.

The Thompson family are worthy successors to the Bickerstaffe dynasty, and in 1922 the Pleasure Beach was described as 'the earthly paradise of a shrewd, hard-working people'. Having run this successful enterprise for four generations, the Thompson family have all been recognised for their contribution to seaside entertainment. Geoffrey, his mother Doris, and daughter Amanda have all been awarded the OBE, an honour that William George Bean would have been extremely proud of.

Geoffrey Thompson was also active in public life, having been appointed Deputy Lieutenant of Lancashire and school governor, as well as supporting various charitable trusts. Both Geoffrey and his father Leonard appear in the Hall of Fame of the International Association of Amusement Parks and Attractions, along with the names of Walt Disney and George Ferris, the inventor of the giant fairground wheel. Amanda Thompson, William Bean's great-granddaughter, is now the managing director of the Pleasure Beach. She is also president of the company Stageworks Worldwide Productions, who have been staging live ice shows since 1982, a director of the Big Blue Hotel and patron of both the Grand Theatre and Blackpool Civic Trust.

## Into the Twenty-first Century

The twenty-first century has brought the park many accolades, both for its rides and the park itself. Voted the fifth best amusement park in the world and the UK's best amusement park in 2017, it was the most visited tourist attraction in the country. Valhalla, constructed in June 2000 at a cost of £15 million, was voted best water ride in the world for the fifth year running. More recently, the Icon was voted one of the best new roller coasters in Europe.

The last few years have seen major investment into luxury hotels in the resort. Long gone are the days when the Blackpool landlady reigned supreme.

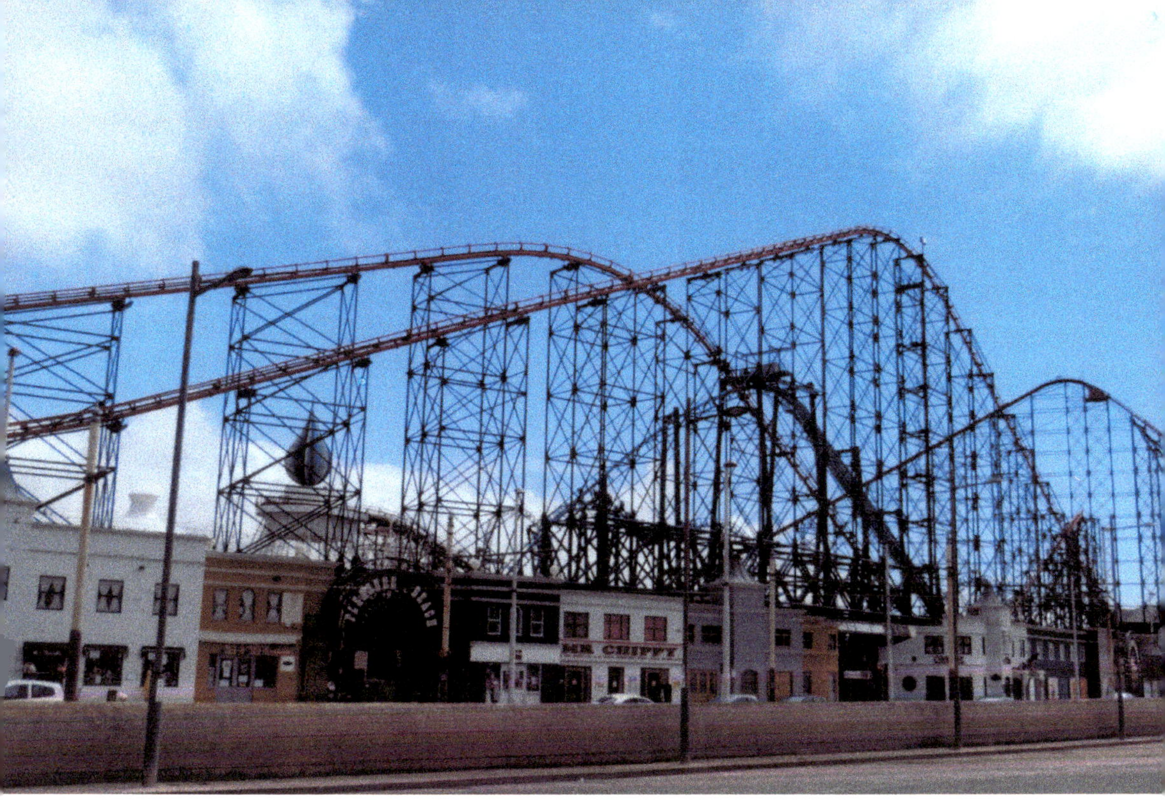

The Big One roller coaster.

The latest addition to the Pleasure Beach's portfolio is the Boulevard, a 120-room, £12 million hotel that opened in November 2018. It is situated near the Big Blue Hotel, which has been operating since August 2003, the first venture of its kind for the Pleasure Beach Company.

Thanks to William George Bean's vision, his legacy continues with four generations of his family who continue to thrill the public throughout the summer season and beyond.

## Seven Miles of Golden Sands

Prior to 1916 the beach was said to be the 'happy hunting ground of cheap-jacks, phrenologists, ventriloquists, ice-cream and oyster vendors, sweetmeat dealers and traders of all kinds'. This led to bylaws coming into force that enabled the corporation to sweep away what they considered to be the most objectionable of these establishments. The beach traders were now subject to stringent regulations. The whole extent of the foreshore, an area extending seawards for 185 yards from the sea wall, was reserved for private traders, who purchased annual permits from the corporation by auction. A space 50 yards wide on each side of the three piers to the low-water mark was to be free of any traders. Outside this area the sands were free for anyone wishing to do business on the beach. Competition was so

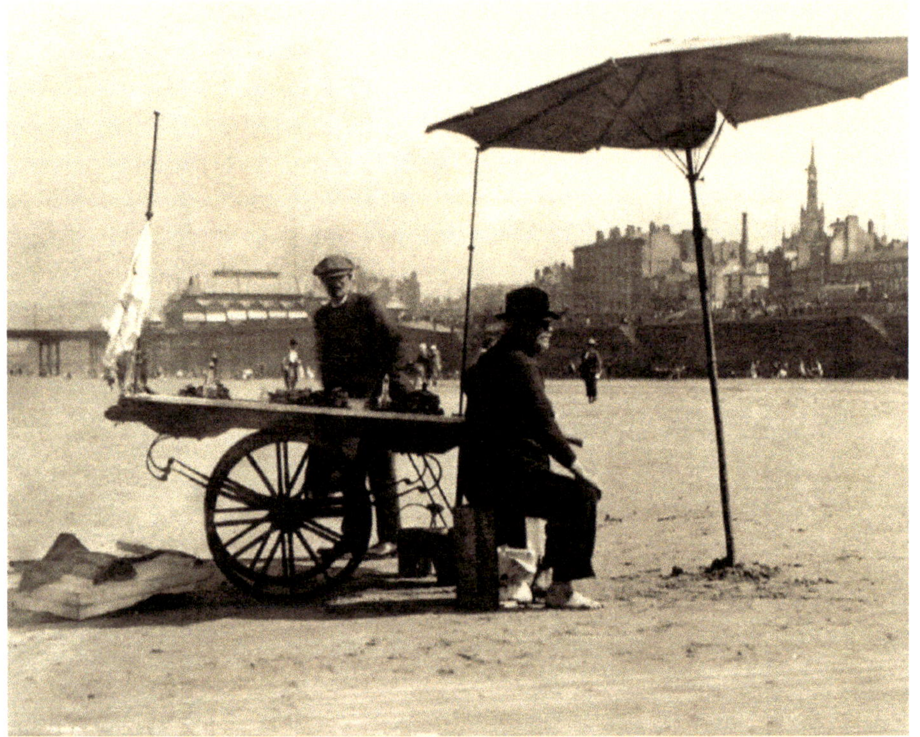

Oyster sellers on the beach.

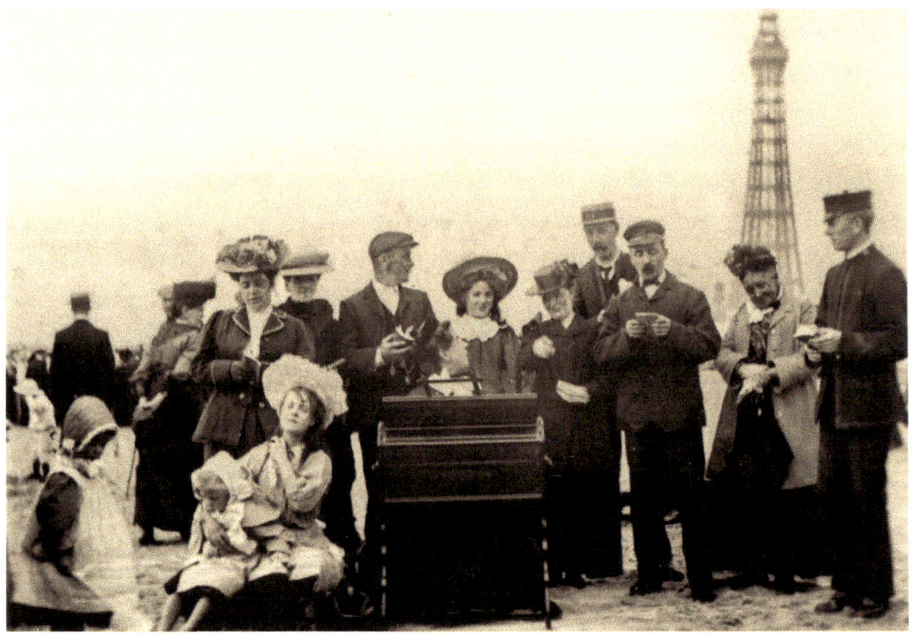

Singers on the beach.

fierce for stalls that prices shot up; in 1921 an ice-cream vendor was said to have paid the record sum of £500 for a single stall and more than £10,000 was netted for the sale of fewer than 100 licences.

Together with its oyster, cockles and whelk stalls, buckets and spades, and seaside entertainers, Blackpool was seen as the affordable getaway for families throughout the late nineteenth and early twentieh centuries.

The arrival of donkeys on Britain's beaches in the 1880s, first seen in Margate, proved so popular they spread all over the country. It is believed that donkey rides first operated in Blackpool in 1890. The earliest postcard shows them in 1901 and they are still popular to this day.

Punch and Judy celebrated 350 years in 2019. Another operator, whose family entertained visitors for several generations, was Professor Green. At one time there were as many as nine separate Punch and Judy shows being staged by the Greens along the stretch of Blackpool sands. (Punch and Judy operators have traditionally

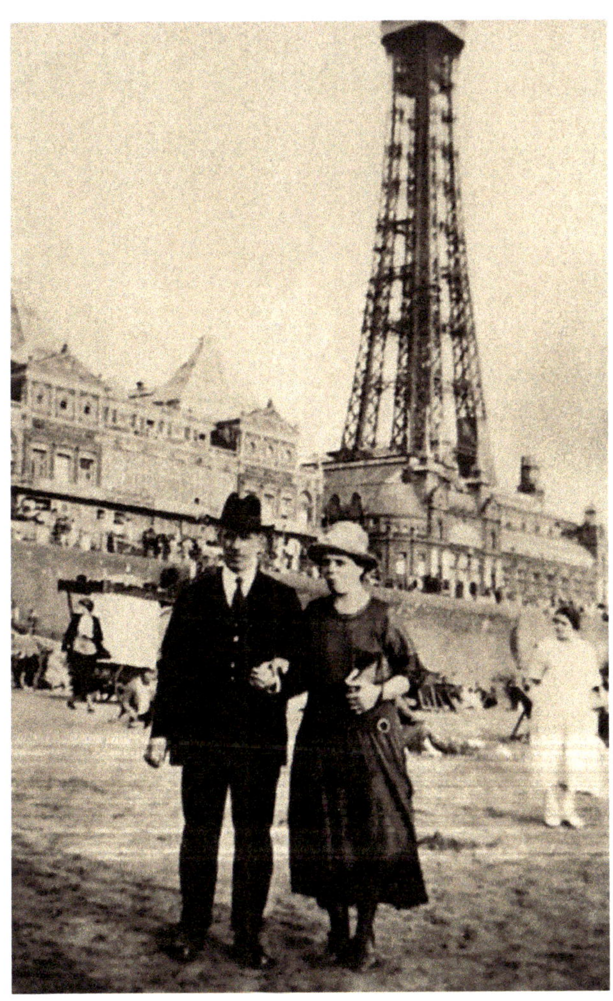

Mr and Mrs Martin.

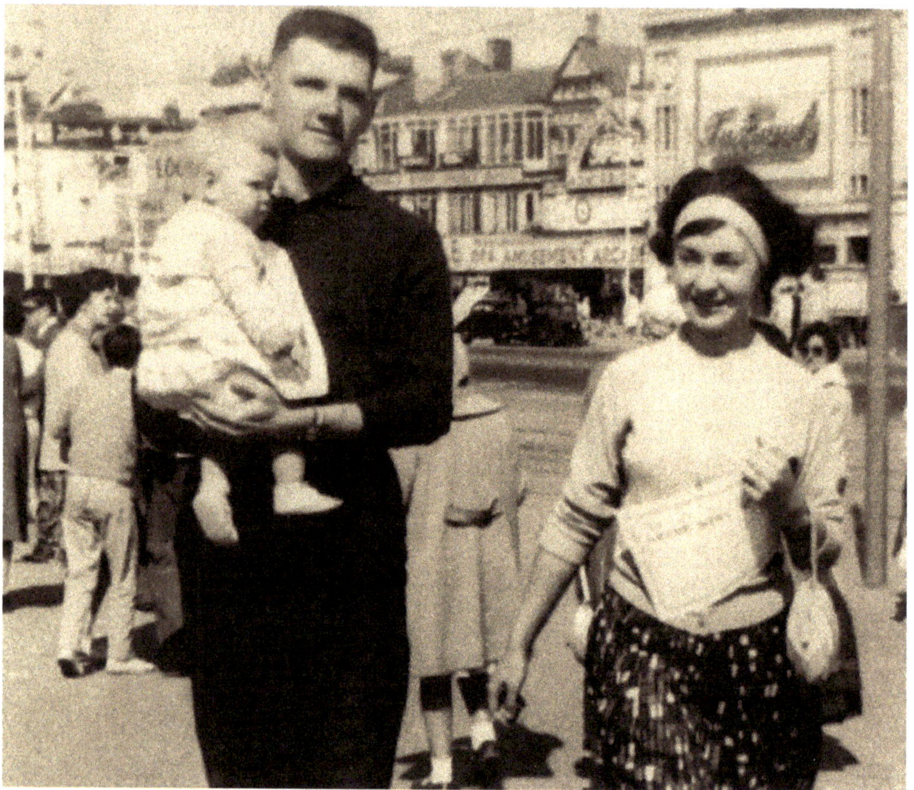

Holidaymakers, 1962.

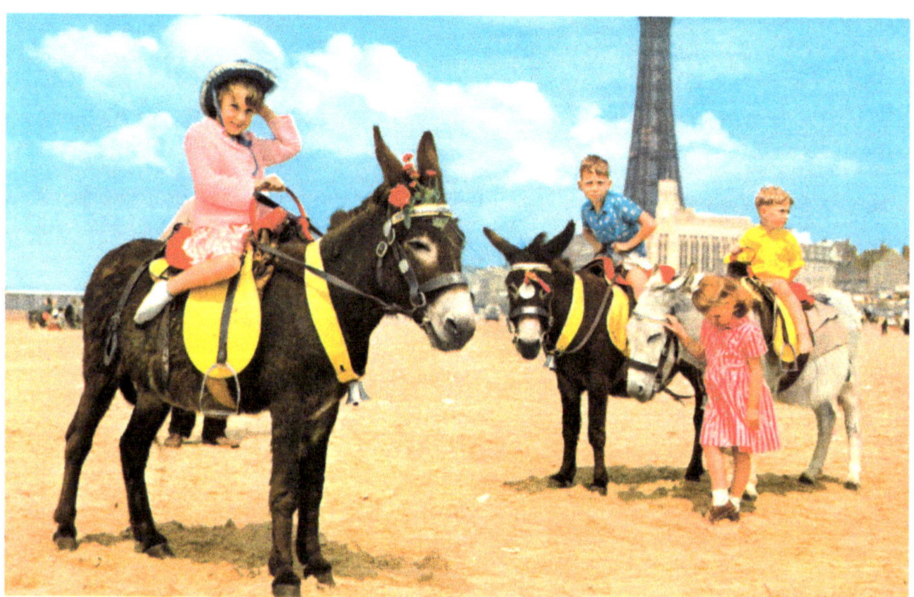

Donkeys on the beach.

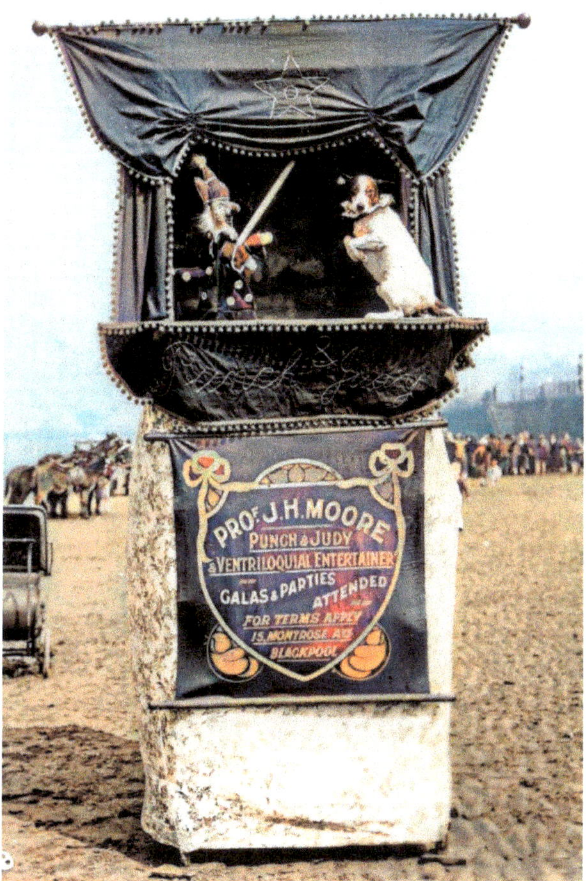


Punch and Judy show
*Professor Moore.*

referred to themselves as professors.) The last Professor Green retired as recently as the 1980s and passed away in 2020 at the age of ninety-five. Although there are now probably only a handful of resorts left with a resident Punch and Judy on the beach, promenade or pier, the show's popularity has never waned. Still, it is now more likely to be found at private venues than at the end of the pier. Blackpool professional magician and puppeteer Martin Scott-Price is keeping the tradition alive in the resort for future generations by opening a museum in General Street showcasing a vast display of puppets and Punch and Judy memorabilia.

# Blackpool's Iconic Hotels and Hostelries

Before the coming of the railways in the mid-nineteenth century, travelling to Blackpool would have been a long and arduous journey. The first stagecoach service was established in 1781 during the summer. Visitors to Blackpool at the time were described as Lancashire gentry, merchants and manufacturers and needed somewhere to stay. In the late 1780s there were only around fifty houses in the town. To fulfil this need for accommodation, Lawrence Bailey, a farmer from the area, built the Metropole Hotel, which was completed around 1785. Situated in a prominent position on the northern shoreline, it was at the time one of only four hotels in the burgeoning resort. Of these four hotels only two now remain: Bailey's Hotel (which became the Metropole later) and the Clifton Arms (now operating under its original name, Forshaws).

## Bailey's Hotel (Metropole)

Bailey's Hotel boasted thirty-four bedrooms, three dining rooms, and a coffee lounge. After several changes of name and ownership, during which time it was known as the Higher Royal Hotel and then the Rossall's Dickson Hotel, by 1867 it had reverted to its original name of Bailey's. When the first stretch of promenade was opened in 1856, running from the hotel to the Houndshill area, the hotel was situated in an enviable position. With the arrival of the trams in 1885, the first section of track was laid directly outside the hotel, making it even more accessible. It remains the only hotel situated on the seaward side of the tram track.

After extensive renovations and additions, including shops on the landward side, the hotel was renamed Hotel Metropole, as it is still known today. At the turn of the century, the hotel had doubled in size and boasted lavish interiors, with both suites and bedrooms, a Moorish-style lounge, a Louis XV-style drawing room, and a Georgian-style dining room. In 1955, it was purchased by the Butlin's holiday chain, who maintained ownership until 1998 when it was sold to the Grand Hotels chain, who changed the name to Grand Metropole

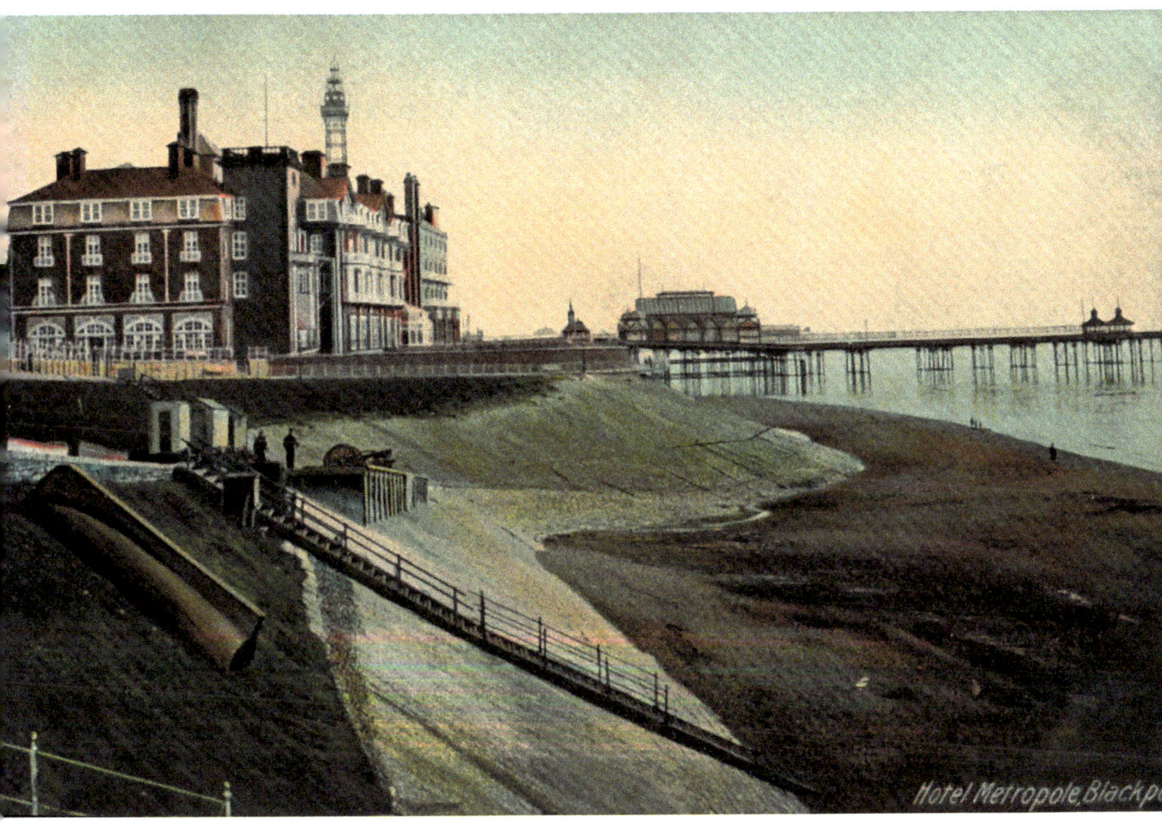



Hotel Metropole.

Blackpool. Taken over by Britannia Hotels in 2004, it now has a total of 223 bedrooms, two restaurants, and a café, with stunning tranquil views across the Irish Sea.

## Forshaws (Clifton Arms Hotel)

The only other hotel operating today that dates back to the time of Bailey's Hotel is the Clifton Hotel in Talbot Square, which stands on the site of one of the four oldest hotels, dating from the 1780s. Originally called Forshaws, it was sold to Thomas Clifton in 1843 and renamed the Clifton Arms Hotel. It was partly demolished and reconstructed in 1865. The original brick facing with stone dressing has since been stuccoed and rendered. In its heyday, it held the best location, facing the sea, opposite the North Pier and near to all the major amenities. In 1971, it had ninety-four bedrooms, thirty-four with a private bath, and bed and breakfast was £2.55 a day. Awarded Grade II listed status in 1974, this historic hotel was at the centre of the festivities in honour

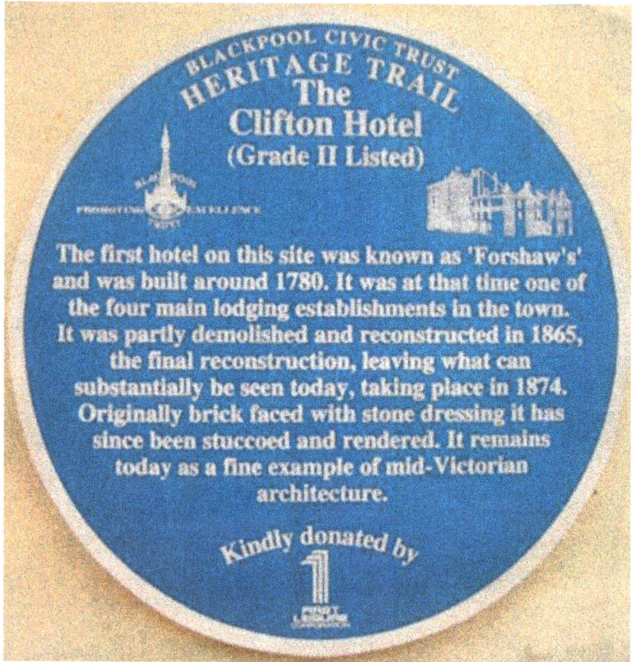



Clifton Hotel blue plaque.

of the opening of North Pier on 22 May 1863. This ninety-room hotel has recently undergone a £400,000 refurbishment and reverted back to its original name of Forshaws Hotel.

## Hydropathic Hotels

With the fashion of water cures and hydrotherapy remedies in the second half of the nineteenth century, hydropathic hotels sprang up in towns and seaside resorts. Advertisements were placed in national newspapers to entice visitors to the 'Brighton of the North', offering 'everything to ensure a perfect bracing holiday'.

### Norbreck Hydro Hotel

The Norbreck Castle Hotel, a prominent feature of North Shore, was originally developed at the turn of the twentieth century from a large, private, country house called Norbreck Villa. It was renamed the Norbreck Hydro and in the 1930s had facilities such as a ballroom, swimming pool and solarium. In 1936, the hotel advertised itself as 'the greatest recreative hydro in the world', with an eighteen-hole golf course, twenty-three tennis courts, a cinema, ballroom, gymnasium, and warm water swimming baths. Decades of development have made it into a 480-bedroom hotel with twenty-two conference suites, and meeting and banqueting rooms, the largest of which can hold 3,000 people.

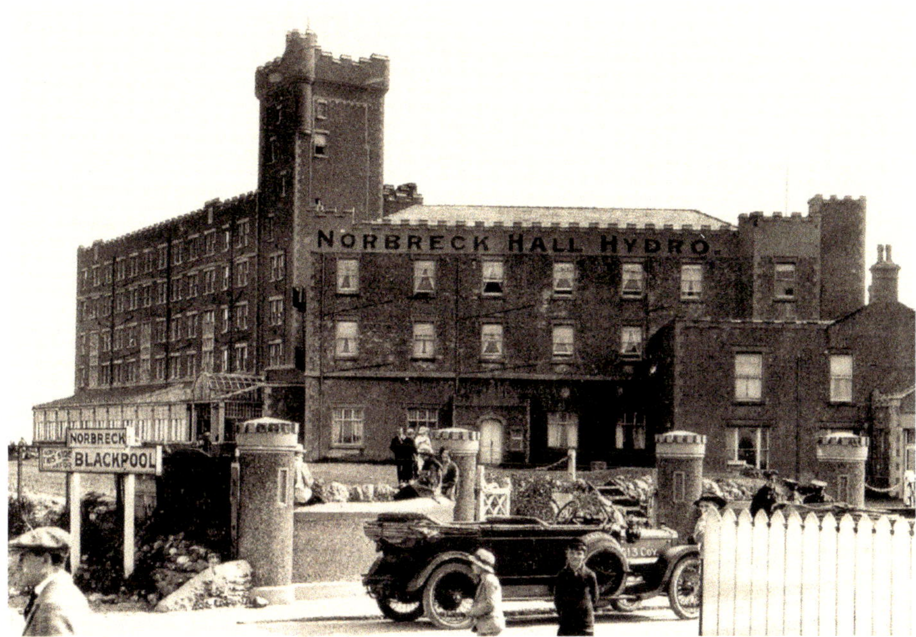


Norbreck Castle Hotel.

### Imperial Hydro Hotel

To attract 'elite' visitors to holiday resorts during the mid-nineteenth century, grand, luxurious and imposing hotels were built all around the coast of England. Dominant among those was the Imperial Hotel, Blackpool, designed by Clegg and Knowles of Manchester. Built of red brick in a French Renaissance and baroque style, it opened in 1867 and the *Yorkshire Post* of 24 November 1873 reported that 'this magnificent hotel is delightfully situated in its own grounds, Claremont Park on the North Cliff, terms very moderate, the cuisine and wines excellent, terms very moderate. Every accommodation combining the quietude and comfort of a home for families and gentlemen'.

In the early days it was a temperance hotel, and it was not until prohibition of alcohol was lifted that the hotel became successful. Positioned on the Promenade, this hydropathic establishment built at a cost of £50,000 was said by the German-British art and architectural historian Nikolaus Pevsner to be 'the climax of Blackpool *hotelerie*'. Toll gates were erected at Lansdowne Terrace and Gynn Square to control access to the Promenade. Pedestrians had to pay one penny, and carriages were charged 3*d* for admission.

Its opulent interior included the Palm Court Restaurant, Louis XVI room and ballroom with a glass ceiling, and a Turkish, Russian and seawater bath complex in the basement. Such was the magnificence of the hotel that it hosted the official opening of the Winter Gardens in 1878 and was also the venue for a grand gala dinner to celebrate the laying of the foundations of Blackpool Tower in 1891.

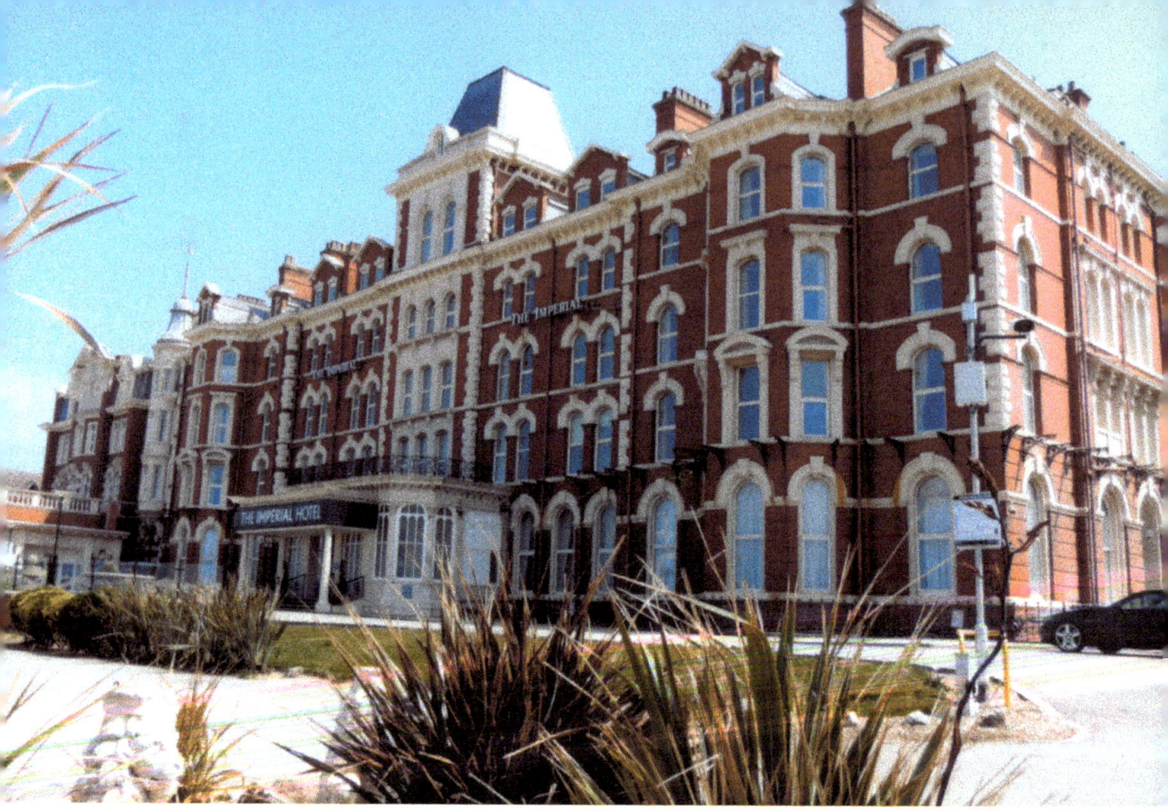

*Above*: Imperial Hotel.

*Below*: Claremont Park.

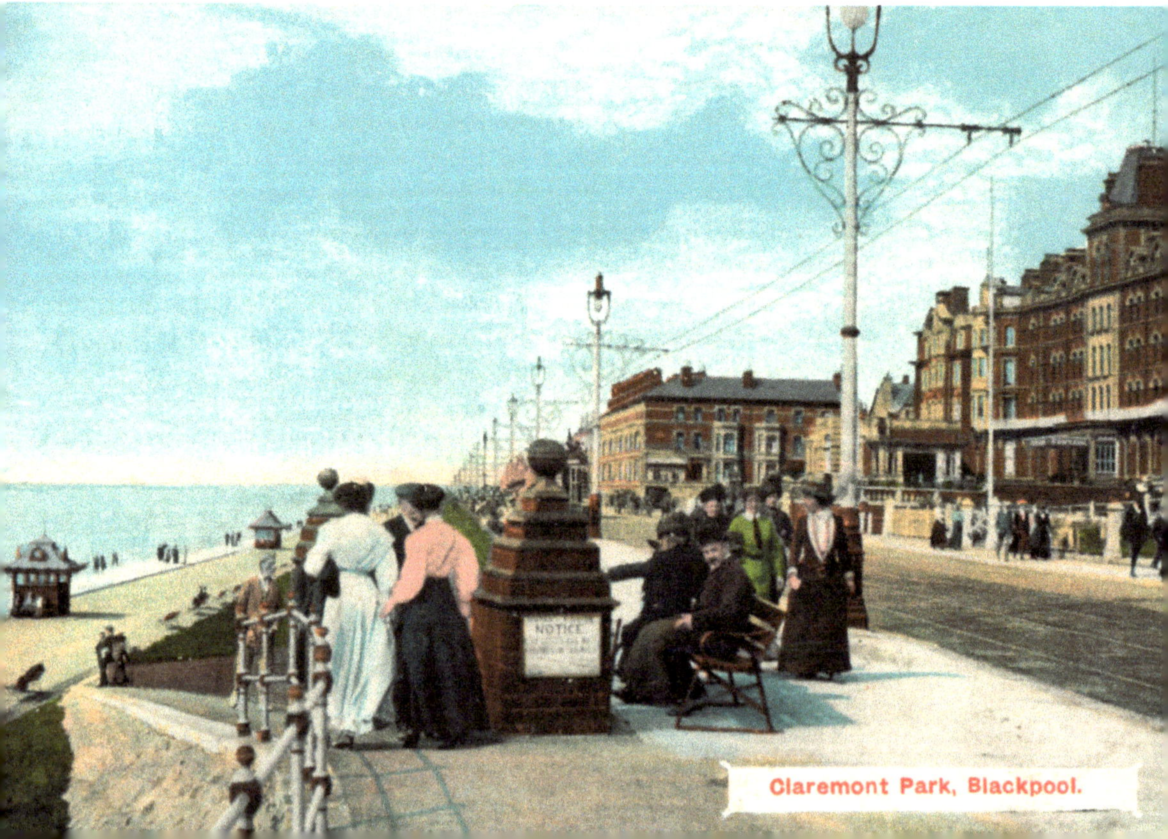

In 1904, an extension to the north wing was a large, neo-baroque-style dining room. The first member of the royal family to stay at the hotel – in Room 311 – was Princess Louise, on the opening of Princess Parade in 1912. Her Majesty the Queen Mother, Princess Margaret and Princess Anne have also stayed in what became known as the Balmoral Suite. Two years after it opened, Charles Dickens came to stay to recover from nervous exhaustion. He wrote enthusiastically of 'this charming sea beach hotel' and his 'delicious walk by the sea'.

In the 1950s, considered to be the golden age of show business in Blackpool, the Imperial welcomed some of the world's famous faces, such as Arthur Askey, Petula Clark, Charlie Drake, Bruce Forsyth, George Melly, Eric Sykes, Tommy Steele, Thora Hird, and Gracie Fields. It also attracted international stars like Errol Flynn, Fred Astaire, and Jayne Mansfield. The Beatles also stayed there in 1964, and on display in the hotel is a photo showing John, Paul and Ringo on one of the sofas before they went on stage at the Winter Gardens to introduce their new film *A Hard Day's Night*.

The Imperial was once an important venue for holding political conferences, Winston Churchill being the first serving prime minister to do so, and he is commemorated in the Churchill Room and Suite (Room 218). In 1985, Margaret Thatcher celebrated her sixtieth birthday at the Imperial. The last major conference in Blackpool was held at the Winter Gardens in 2007, when the Conservatives came to the resort. The original glass-roofed room retains its stained-glass canopy but has been turned into a bar and named No. 10, after all the prime ministers who have served in the UK.

In the 1960s and 1970s modernisation of the hotel meant that much of the original features were hidden or destroyed, but August 2017 saw the successful conclusion of a three-year-long project of restoration. Blackpool Civic Trust volunteers removed the thick plaster and exposed the famous Burmantofts tiles in the Turkish baths, which had disappeared during previous major refurbishments, and gave them a thorough clean, bringing them back to life. This restoration work resulted in the trust and the Imperial Hotel receiving Blackpool Town Council's Conservation Award. This historic hotel, now just as popular as it has always been, serves as a reminder of Blackpool's heyday. Now with modern facilities, a popular restaurant, health club, conference facilities and heritage afternoon teas, its legacy continues into the twenty-first century.

## Hostelries Past and Present

### Foxhall – From Hunting Lodge to Fun Pub

Not all public houses in Blackpool started off as licenced premises. One of the earliest buildings of any substance was Fox Hall, built in 1660 by old Lancashire Royalist Edward Tyldesley and passed down to his son, the diarist Thomas, who lived at Foxhall until his death in 1715. Originally a hunting lodge or summer residence, it became dilapidated by the 1780s. Its eastern end became a farm, while the seaward end became a lodging house. In the 1800s it was extended to become a public house. Between 1840 and 1855, mine host was Richard Caton. Ownership was then passed to Tom Lockwood, who added a concert hall. In

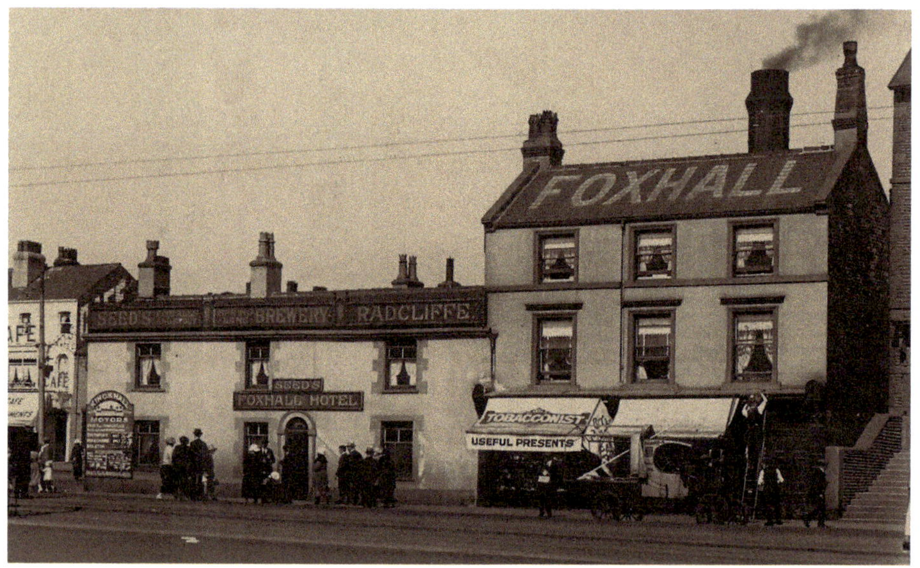

*Above*: Seeds Foxhall Hotel.

*Below*: Modern view of Foxhall Hotel.

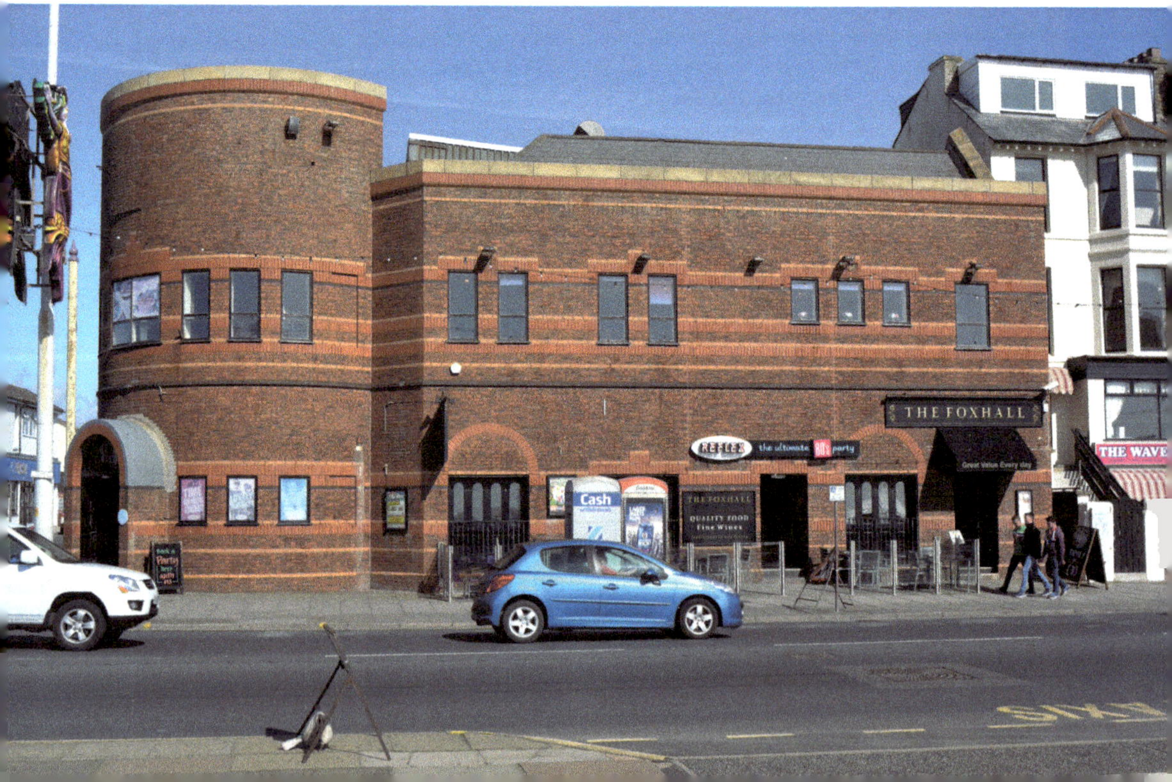

1890, the venue was bought by the Seed family, who held the property until February 1964 when it was sold to C&S Brewery. It suffered a fire in 1955, but parts of the original hall survived in the fabric of the replacement building. It remained a public house until its demolition in 1990, at which time the south bay, facing the sea, was found to have been part of a cobbled building running west to east. Today, a modern, red-brick building exists on the site, housing a popular family pub.

### Saddle Inn – Blackpool's Oldest Public House

The Saddle Inn is Blackpool's oldest public house. Once at the heart of the agricultural community, it dates back to around 1776, when it was owned by Richard Hall, a saddler. At the time it was built Blackpool was just a hamlet in the township of Layton-with-Warbrick. The name Blackpool only began appearing on maps during the mid-eighteenth century. The well-known Leigh family were landlords from 1892 until Jim 'the Beekeeper', who sold pure honey on the premises from his own beehives kept at the rear of the building, retired in 1867. Still operating as a traditional historic inn, it is now the oldest continuously licenced hostelry in Blackpool.

Saddle Inn.

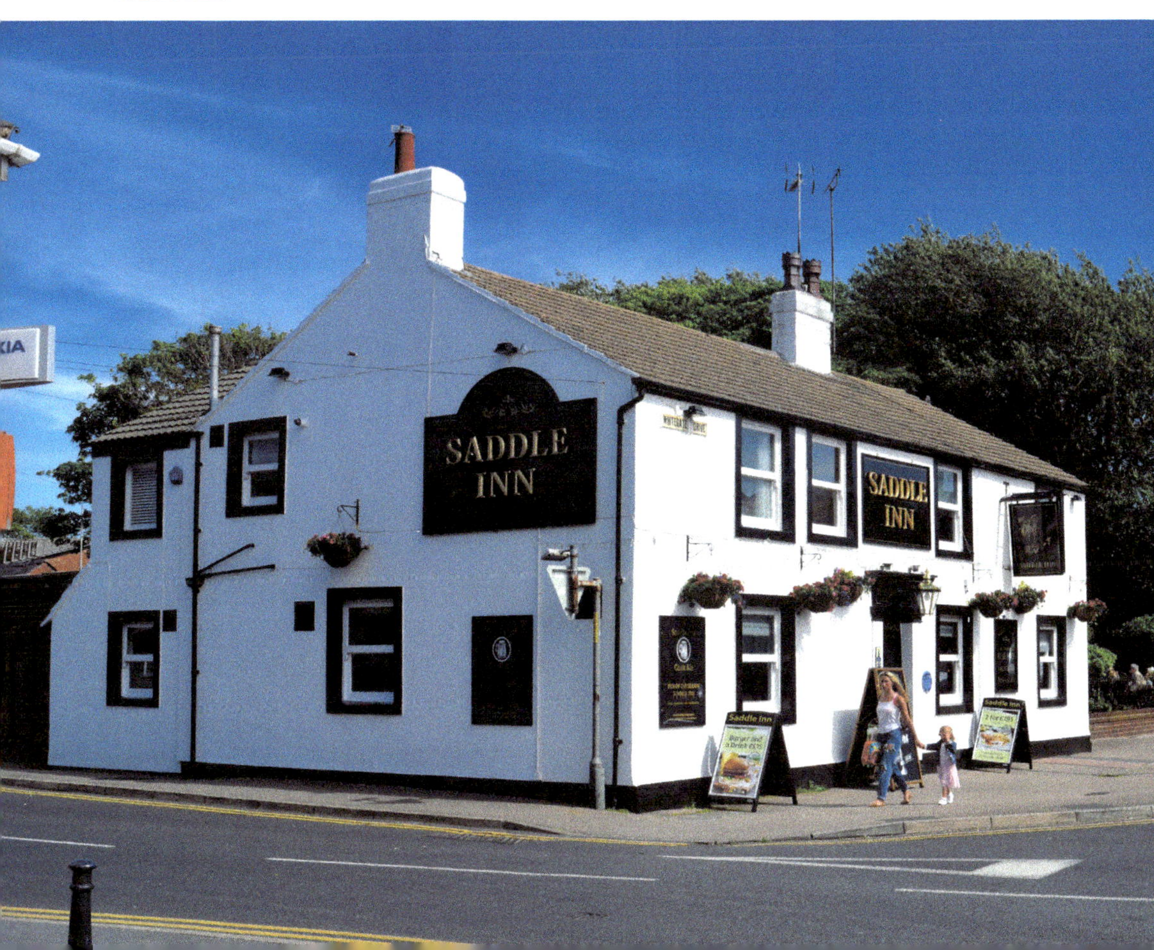

One of the most popular public houses to have existed in Blackpool is the Manchester Hotel. The original building dates back to 1845 when it was known as Manchester House. It was built at the end of the new drive from South Shore (Broad Lane, at the end of the Tullet estate). Spen Dyke, which was a stream of dark water discoloured by peat, discharged into the sea just to the north of the hotel. The new hotel was described as having 'three spacious rooms, ten single bedrooms, and five double bedrooms, above stairs, two with spacious bay windows, commanding good views, also top room, Brewhouse, coach house, stable etc'.

After a major storm in 1852 the bowling greens attached to the hotel were completely destroyed and the bridge, known locally as 'Black Brook', was washed away. In the 1860s the then owner, James Hemingway, renamed it Hemingway's Manchester Hotel. By the early 1880s, however, it had been changed back to the Manchester Hotel.

The hotel was completely rebuilt and opened on 30 May 1936 on what was then known as Manchester Square. Built in an attractive art deco style by the brewers Catterall and Swarbrick, its façade featured four striking vertical fins and sides made of blue brick and a distinctive, tall flagpole. Due to excessive erosion it was rebuilt again in 1996 by Bass Breweries. Now a modern red-brick building, it is one of the most renowned public houses on the Promenade.

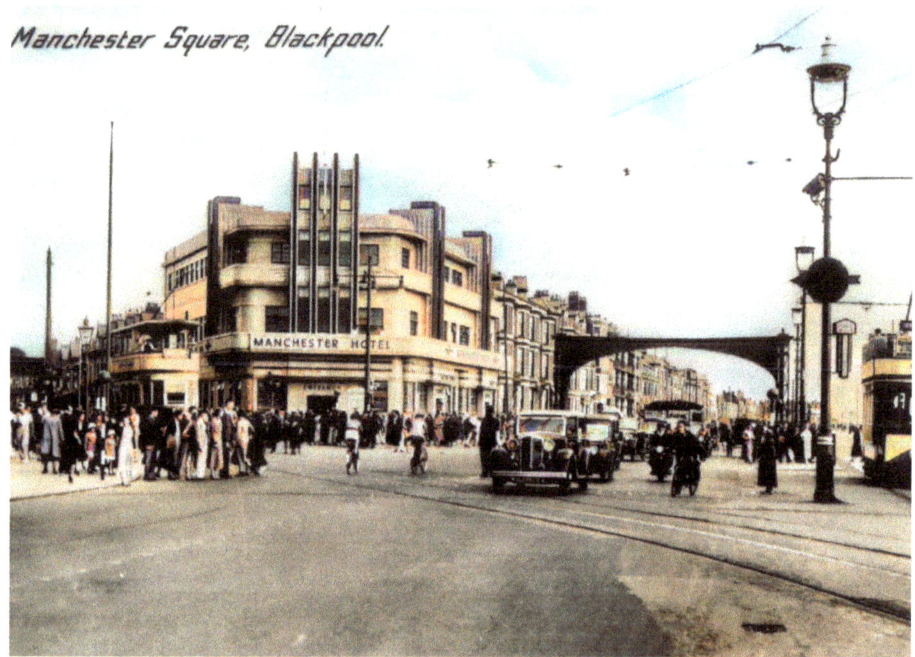


Art deco Manchester Hotel.

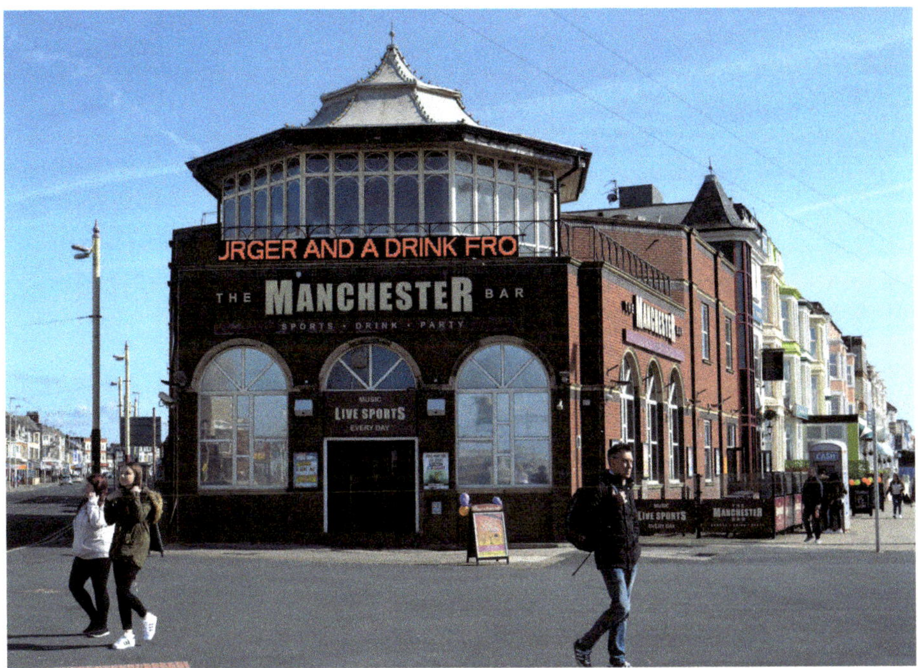


Modern view of Manchester Hotel.

### Halfway House

On 24 September 2019, a historic inn situated on Squires Gate Lane, South Shore, reopened following a £1.8 million refurbishment. The Halfway House, situated halfway between Blackpool and St Annes, is situated on the site of the original inn. A plaque on the wall states that it was built by Ezebiel Salthouse around 1835 as a place where carriages would stop for refreshment as they arrived on Blackpool's borders. After various landlords, it was sold to brewer Matthew Brown in 1874. It was still known as the Halfway House when the brewery constructed the present building, which opened in 1909. Matthew Brown was taken over by Scottish and Newcastle Brewers and the current owners are Enterprise Inns.

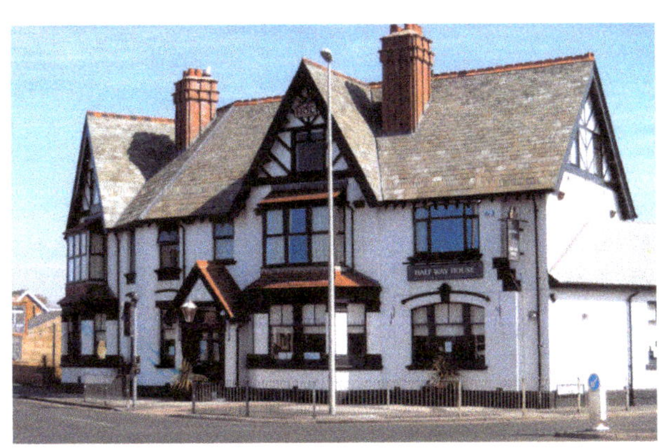

Half Way House.

# Public Houses for the Twenty-first Century

Albert and the Lion

To cater for a new generation of visitors to the resort in the last few years, large breweries have opened public houses with names that have historical connections to Blackpool.

Since 2010 Wetherspoon's have opened three public houses, the first of which was the Albert and the Lion, situated on Bank Hey Street, first operating in July of that year. Converted from a former Woolworths store, designed in the art deco style, it takes its name from a famous comic monologue written by Marriott Edgar in 1932, immortalised on record by Stanley Holloway. Albert refers to a 'little lad swallowed whole' by a lion in the menagerie at the bottom of the Tower. Woolworths was referred to as the shop where Albert had purchased 'a stick with an 'orse's head handle, the finest that money could buy' with which he had prodded the beast. Part of the pub's décor is a wooden sculpture of a lion's head on the wall of the bar, with Albert in the lion's mouth.

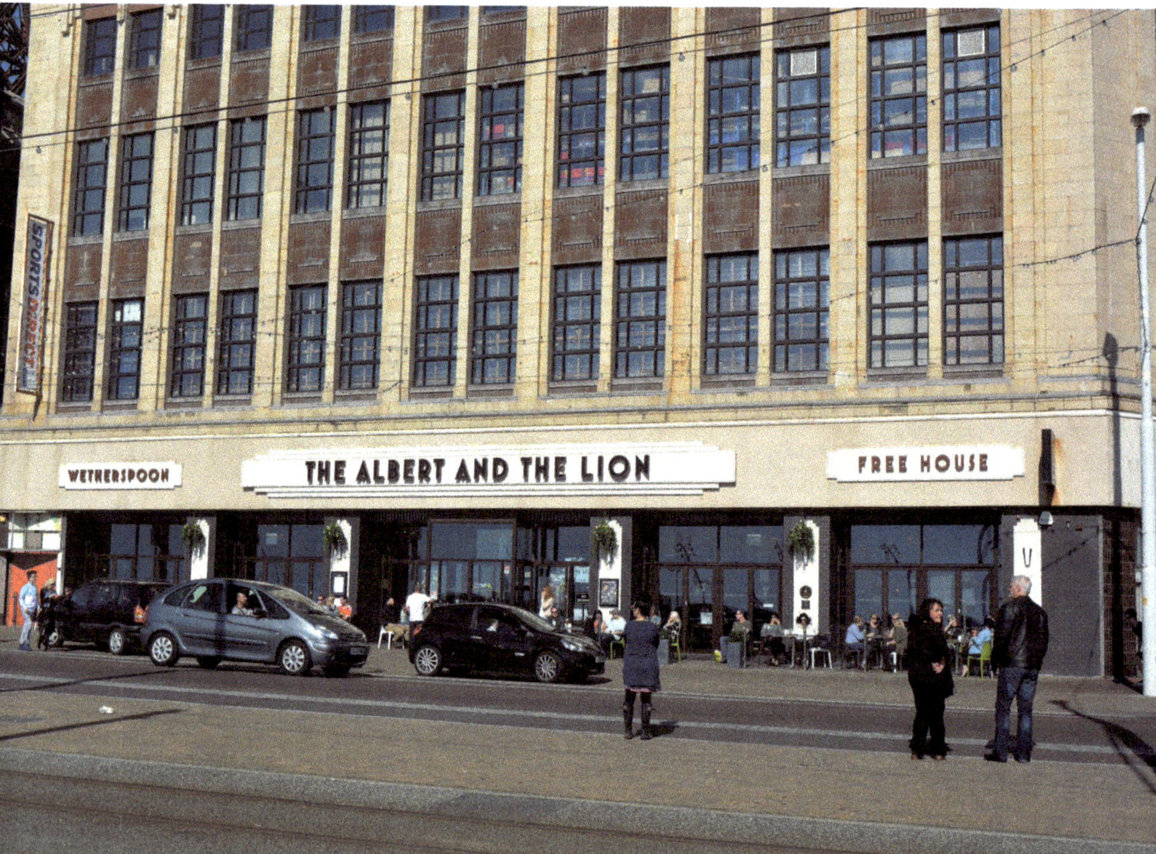


Albert and the Lion public house.

### The Layton Raikes

The unusual name of the Layton Raikes – a pub located in Market Street and built over two floors with a roof terrace, which opened in 2011 – is taken from the original name of the area, which was connected to the sea via a 'rake' – a Scandinavian word for 'path'. From the late nineteenth century the site was occupied by Whiteheads Fish, Game, Poultry and Oyster Warehouse. It was once part of the Forshaw estate, which gave its name to an earlier hotel, Forshaws (now the Clifton Hotel). Inside the pub are many artefacts depicting the history of Blackpool and in the downstairs bar is an illuminated sculpture of Tower Circus clown Charlie Cairolli, a large mural depicting local landmark buildings, fixed seating in the style of a waltzer, a carousel horse, and fun house-style mirrors.

### The Velvet Coaster

Situated in a prominent seafront position on South Shore near the Pleasure Beach is one of Blackpool's newest public houses, the Velvet Coaster, which opened on 12 May 2015 on the site of the former Lucky Star Amusement Arcade. It is named after the historic Velvet Coaster roller coaster ride, so named because of the open carriages lined with seats covered in velvet. One of the biggest public houses in Britain, it has a large glass frontage and is built on three floors, providing exceptional views of the sea. Its interior is inspired by elements of the sea and roller coasters. The pub is decorated with many Blackpool artefacts, a selection of vintage Blackpool theatre posters, a huge wickerwork sculpture of a circus strongman, and a timeline celebrating the town's history.

Velvet Coaster public house.

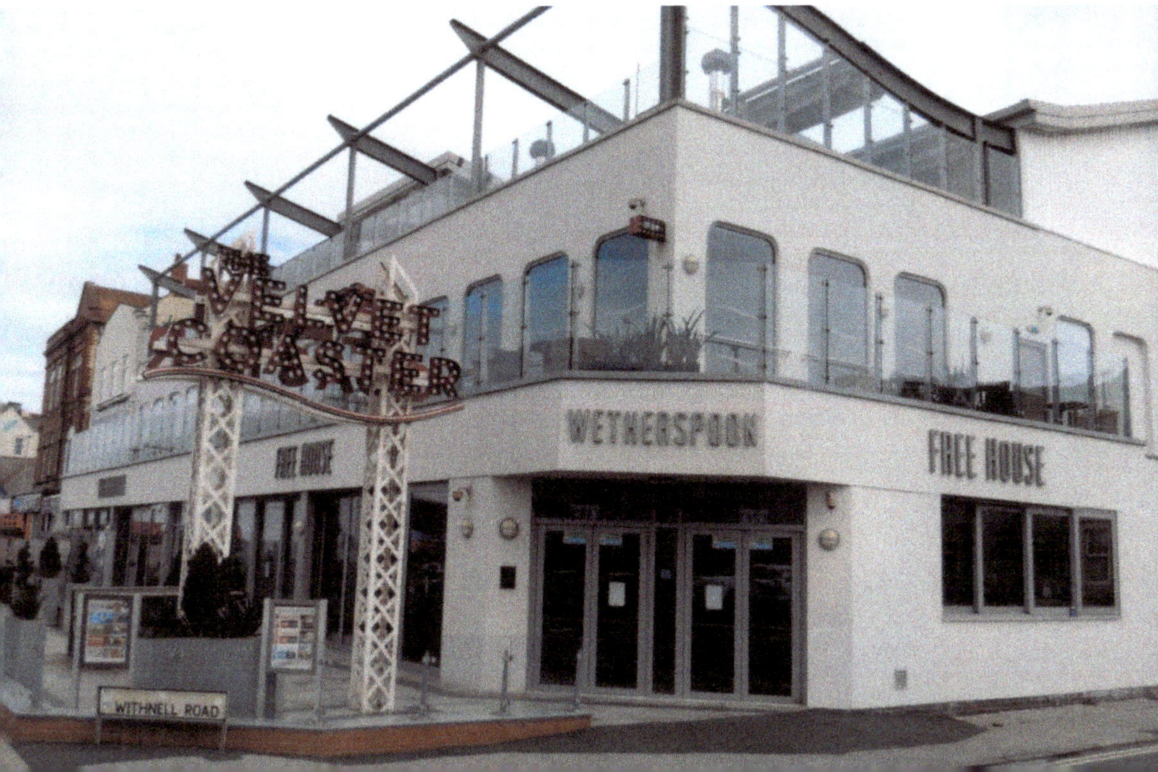

# 7
# Culture and Leisure

## Cuthbert and John Grundy and the Establishment of the Grundy Art Gallery

A modest commemorative stone set in the wall of the Recreation Ground in South Shore bears a dedication to a man called Cuthbert Grundy. Known as Grundy Memorial Park, these grounds once housed Highfield Library, donated in 1914 by Cuthbert and his brother John Grundy, who owned the land on which the recreational park sat.

A far more elaborate tribute in the form of a bust of St Cuthbert Cartwright Grundy, presented by public subscription to the Corporation of Blackpool in 2007, stands the Grundy Art Gallery in Queen Street. When the two brothers (born in Bury to a wealthy Unitarian family) settled in Blackpool, they were to

Blackpool Central Library.

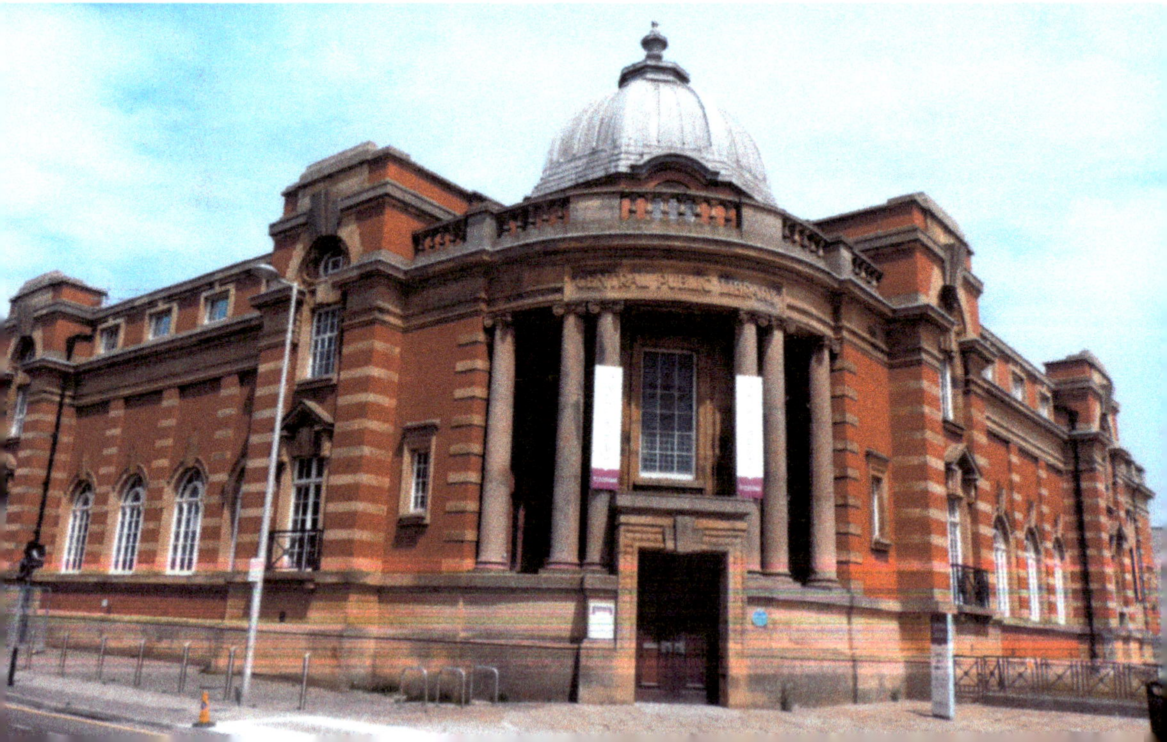

make a significant contribution to the arts in their adopted town. Talented amateur painters of figures and landscapes, they both threw themselves wholeheartedly into promoting the arts, holding exhibitions and events, and founding the Painting and Sketching Society, which was the forerunner of Blackpool Arts Society.

Exhibiting at the Royal Academy and Walker Gallery, the Grundy brothers recognised the need for an art gallery in Blackpool to exhibit their paintings and provide opportunities for other local and national artists. To this end they financed a building in Queen Street, which was to become the Grundy Art Gallery. It opened on 26 October 1911, and over the coming years the brothers made a generous donation of some of their best works. When reporting the opening ceremony of the library and art gallery, the *Manchester Courier* of 27 October referred to Cuthbert and John Grundy as 'two wealthy South Shore gentlemen who have done much to foster a love of art in Blackpool'.

Their generosity, however, extended far beyond the arts. Their Unitarian dedication to the cause of equality and care for others resulted in them opening a convalescent home for children at No. 238 Stony Hill Avenue, which became known as Stonyhill Children's Centre when it was taken over by Blackpool Corporation. Cuthbert held Unitarian Sunday services in the sitting room of his home, Grundy House, in Lytham Road, before the opening of the South Shore Unitarian Tin Tabernacle in 1894. In November 1902, the foundation stones of the new South Shore Church were laid, the ceremony being carried out by leaders of the South Shore movement, Mr and Mrs J. R. Grundy and Mr C. C. Grundy.

Cuthbert Grundy's generosity, kindness and philanthropy earned him a knighthood awarded by George V granting him the honour of being the first man in Blackpool to be ennobled. He also became a Justice of the Peace (JP), and in his eighties he was bestowed with the Freedom of Blackpool. Cuthbert Grundy reached a great age, dying months before his 100th birthday at his home for over five decades: Grundy House, No. 456 Lytham Road.

The year 2019 marked the 135th anniversary of the Blackpool Art Society, and to celebrate the impact the brothers had on the artistic community of their time the society held an open art exhibition featuring works from both its current membership and a selection of works made and donated by Cuthbert and John Grundy themselves. In 2021, Grundy Art Gallery celebrated the 110th anniversary of the opening of its doors to the public.

## Blackpool Central Library, a Carnegie Masterpiece

At the entrance to Blackpool Central Library is a dedication plaque marking the occasion of the presentation of the library to the borough of Blackpool. This magnificent building in the Edwardian baroque style was designed by Scottish architectural firm Cullen, Lochhead and Brown. The library, built with funds donated by Scottish/Canadian philanthropist Andrew Carnegie, was officially opened in 1911 by Lord Shuttleworth, Lord Lieutenant of the county. It replaced the former free library in nearby Market Street (now the site of the Municipal Buildings), which opened on 25 March 1895. Awarded Grade II listing in 1983 by English Heritage, the library was closed for a year in 2010 for a £3 million renovation programme. The sum of £2 million was provided by the Big Lottery Fund, and the remaining million from Blackpool Council. The library celebrated its centenary on 26 October 1984 and as part of the renovation, eight new stained-glass windows were commissioned.

A £390,000 renovation to repair the library's leaky roof will ensure that part of Blackpool's rich history will be protected for the future. At a time when many libraries are closing, Blackpool is fortunate to have such a magnificent library, made modern and accessible, yet retaining many of its original Victorian features, including its ornate staircase, which are a testament to its benefactor, Andrew Carnegie.

## Stanley Park, an Oasis of Calm

In the late nineteenth century, town councils laid out public parks for recreation, enabling the public to play sports and enjoy the outdoors in their leisure time. Blackpool was already hugely popular as a holiday resort, and in 1922 it was decided to create a leisure facility that would serve visitors as well as local residents. Away from the holiday crowds along the Promenade and the beach is an oasis of calm and tranquillity: 300 acres of parkland, which was opened to the public on 2 October 1926.

Blackpool's first municipal park was designed by Thomas Mawson on a grand scale, with a boating lake, Italian gardens, and recreational facilities blending architecture and horticulture against a backdrop of natural woodland. An art

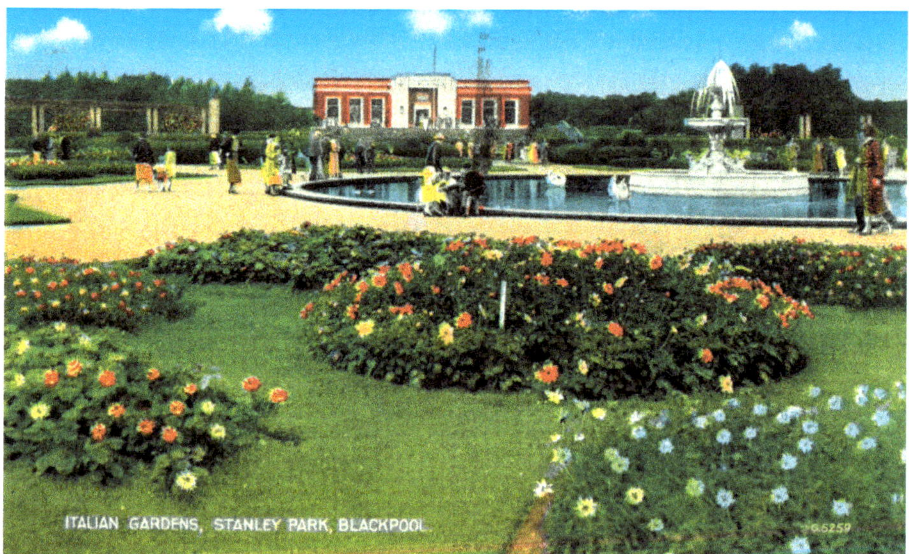


Italian Gardens, Stanley Park.

deco-style café designed by J. C. Robinson, Blackpool's borough architect, was added in 1927, with steps down to a boating lake and an amphitheatre housing a bandstand adding the finishing touches. It even has its own model village depicting scenes from times gone by, recreated in miniature. It was officially opened by Lord Derby, Sir George Edward Villiers Stanley, from whom the park gets its name.

When the park's ninetieth birthday celebrations were held on 8 July 2017, the guest of honour was Earl Stanley (great-grandson of the man who had opened the park in 1926), who ceremoniously opened the gates with a silver key. A procession of civic dignitaries and representatives of local schools in order of founding date, one for each decade, marched to the end of Mawson Drive to the music of the Park Community Academy Band.

An impressive clock tower, a memorial dedicated to Blackpool's first mayor, is flanked by two bronze lion head drinking fountains. The most recent memorial, situated in the memorial garden between the clock tower and the Italian gardens, was unveiled in a private ceremony in memory of a local lady named Jane Tweddle, one of the tragic victims of the Manchester Arena Bombing in 2017.

A group of enthusiastic and dedicated volunteers led by an elected committee, the Friends of Stanley Park and Salisbury Woodland was established on 10 July 2002. Involved in gardening, wildlife conservation and promotional events, they staff the visitor centre, raise funding for projects on the park, and promote and protect the park and woodland for the future. Awarded Grade II listing in 1955, after a major restoration funded by the Lottery Fund in 2007 the park was given a Green Flag Award. Included in the Register of Historic Parks and Gardens of Special Historic Interest in England, it was awarded the title of Best Park in the UK in 2017 and 2019, beating many contenders. In 2022, the Friends have been awarded the accolade of the Queen's Award for Voluntary Service.

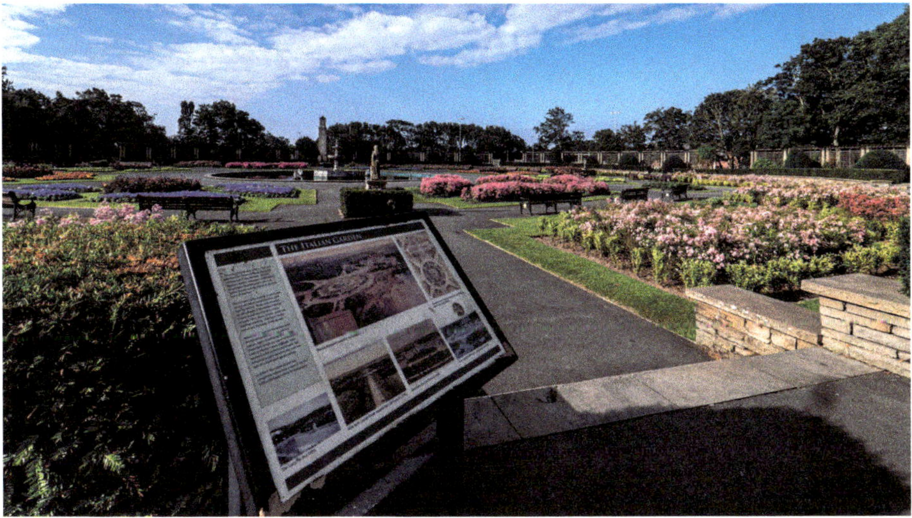

Modern view of Stanley Park.

# Royal Visits

For over a hundred years, Blackpool has welcomed royal visits to the town. The most recent one took place on Tuesday, 1 October 2019, on the occasion of the 125th birthday of two of the town's most iconic landmarks – Blackpool Tower and the Grand Theatre. A blue plaque was unveiled by Sophie, Countess of Wessex, in the Tower to record this historic event and also marked the opening of the new fifth-floor Family Entertainment Suite. Earlier in the year hundreds of people welcomed the then Duke and Duchess of Cambridge to take a look at health and social problems of the town. There they met members of the local community, and a poignant moment for William was when they visited the giant mirror in the Tower, unveiled by his mother Diana, Princess of Wales, in 1992 to mark the opening of Tower World.

The first monarch to pay a visit was George V in 1913, at the celebration of the 50th anniversary of the opening of the North Pier in 1863. During preparations for the visit, a bomb was discovered on the Central Pier by two local children. At first thought to be a hoax, further examination confirmed it was genuine and, recognising the serious consequences of an explosion on the pier, each of the children were rewarded for their diligence with the presentation of a watch and chain.

The Mayor of Blackpool, Councillor Milton G. Wilde, also distributed between 3,000 and 4,000 of the 8,000 medals prepared for local schoolchildren to be worn on the day of the visit. There had been much rejoicing in the town at the time of the coronation of King George and Queen Mary, and children were very much at the forefront of the proceedings as they were given freedom of the town, free tram rides, a gala, and sports. Meanwhile, the adults were treated to an ox roast and a firework display.

When the Duke of Kent opened a new stretch of promenade in 1937, ten thousand schoolchildren cheered him on his way to Little Bispham, where he performed the ceremony by cutting a ribbon with a pair of gold scissors. After opening a new lifeboat house, where he named a new motor lifeboat, he performed the final ceremony of the day by switching on the Illuminations before a 20,000-strong crowd on Talbot Square. At the end of the evening, an illuminated tramcar carried the duke on a tour of the Illuminations.

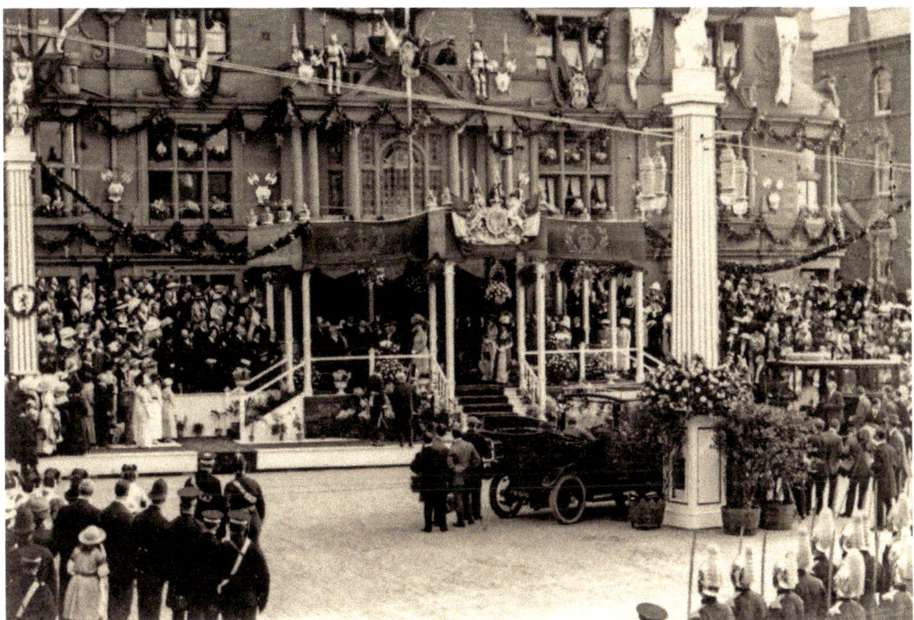

George V outside the Town Hall, 1913.

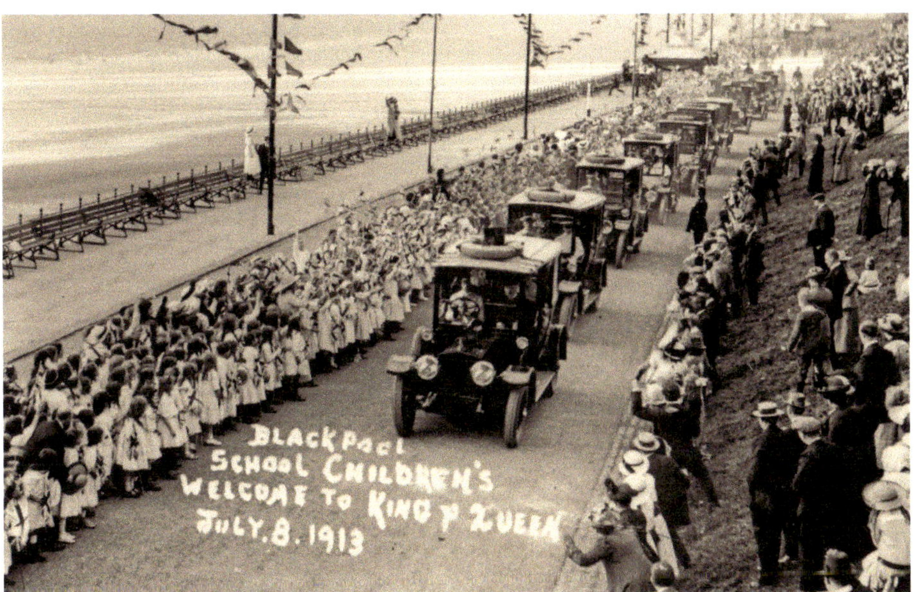



Blackpool schoolchildren welcome the king and queen.

In 1955, Elizabeth II, accompanied by Prince Philip, attended the Royal Variety Performance at the Opera House – the first to be staged outside London. A star-studded performance attracted top celebrities of the day, such as comedy duo Jimmy Jewell and Ben Warriss, George Formby, Arthur Askey, and a couple of up-and-coming comedians called Morecambe and Wise. Reginald Dixon, the famous Tower organist, played his signature tune, 'I Do Like to be Beside the Seaside', on his organ. On this extra special occasion, the application for tickets exceeded twenty times the allocated 3,000. This was probably the most glittering performance attended by royalty, and a special royal box had been constructed in the Opera House for the occasion. To mark the event, the Promenade was illuminated in purple and gold.

The previous year, nearly half a million people gave Princess Margaret a tumultuous welcome on her first visit to Blackpool. Standing shoulder to shoulder along the 7-mile Promenade in bright sunshine, the crowd cheered and waved as the royal car passed, which had brought the princess back from a tour of the Hawker Aircraft Factory at Squires Gate. On 22 July 1994, at the time of the 100th anniversary of Blackpool's famous landmarks, the Tower and the Grand Theatre, Elizabeth II and Prince Philip came to help celebrate Festival 94 by taking part in a guided tour and a trip to the top of the Tower.

Whether it is to celebrate the anniversary of a local landmark, host a Royal Variety Performance, or meet with the ordinary inhabitants, the coming of royalty to the town is always an occasion for celebration.

# 9

# Civic Pride

On 21 January 1876, Blackpool was granted its charter of incorporation and became a municipal borough, before becoming a county borough in 1904 – a status it retained until local government reorganisation in 1974. 'Progress' was chosen as the motto of the town. It now had the right to elect a mayor, and the first one was Dr W. H. Cocker, son of Dr John Cocker and grandson of Henry Banks, the 'Father of Blackpool'. He served a three-year term. The first election was held on 11 April. The council consisted of the mayor and six aldermen, along with 218 councillors representing the wards of the town. A bill passed in 1879 gave the corporation power to spend the equivalent of a *2d* rate on advertising to promote Blackpool as a resort. For many years Blackpool remained the only town allowed to finance its advertising directly from the rates.

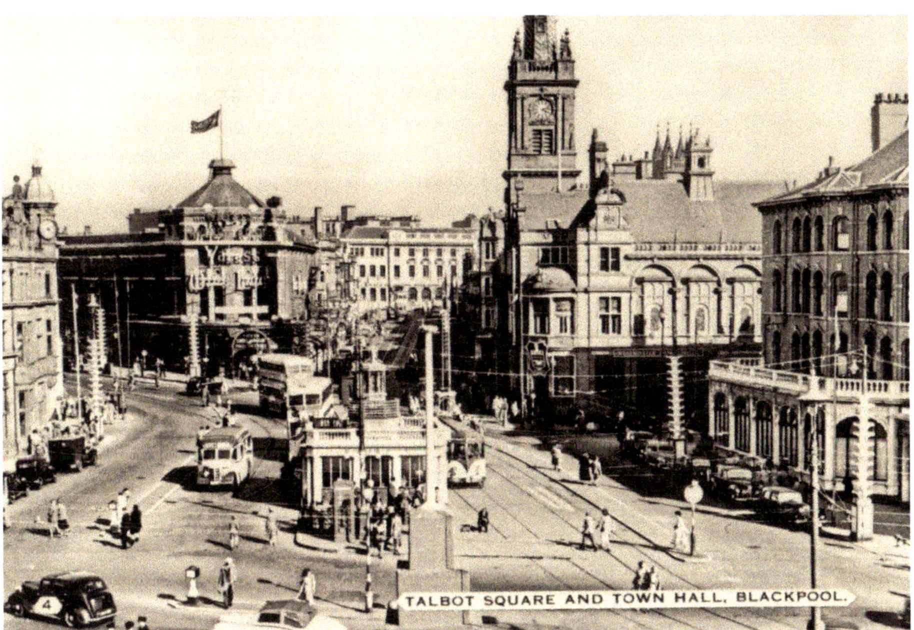


Talbot Square and Town Hall.

Blackpool Town Hall is an imposing structure, built in a Jacobean style between 1895 and 1900. The extension at the rear was added in 1937–38 by the borough architect of the time, Mr J. C. Robinson. It once boasted a magnificent spire topped with a weathervane in the form of a scale model ship. In later years, the spire became unsafe and had to be removed. The interior of the building is equally impressive. The grand staircase in the entrance hall leads to a beautiful stained-glass window, completed in 1900, which contains the coat of arms of Bolton, Manchester, Liverpool, Bury, Oldham, Salford, and Lancaster – all places whose residents frequented Blackpool, making it into the popular resort it is today. The harp of Ireland and the lion rampant of Scotland are also shown, representing the people of those countries that also visited Blackpool in large numbers. At the bottom of the window is the coat of arms of Blackpool, granted by the College of Heralds on 10 June 1899.

There are four windows in the Council Chamber (replaced in the 1940s after the originals were damaged), representing the activities for which Blackpool is known: education, light Industry, agriculture and sport and recreation. In the public gallery is a window from 1900 depicting a seaside scene. The original town badge was donated by the Cocker family in 1876 and depicted a lifeboat, sailing ship, bathing hut and a pier, but was never formally adopted as the town's coat of arms. It was replaced by today's crest in June 1899. Three members of the Bickerstaffe family who were all key players in the growth of the resort served as councillors, and John Bickerstaffe, the driving force in the development of the Tower served as mayor from 1889 to 1891. His younger brother, Thomas, also served as mayor from 1925 to 1926.

In 1922–23, the Mayor of Blackpool was Councillor H. Brooks, a former international gymnast who had first visited the town as a circus performer in 1881. Having suffered an accident, he gave up the circus life and returned to Blackpool in 1887 with his wife to run the Adelphi Hotel on Church Street. Dedicated to politics and charity work, he attended the ceremony in the Tower when Lloyd George was presented with the honorary Freedom of the Borough.

On 21 January 1926, to celebrate the jubilee of its incorporation as a borough, 11,100 schoolchildren were presented with a commemorative card and a box of chocolates. Plans were also made for the erection of a clock tower with a drinking fountain in the new Stanley Park as a suitable memorial for the late Dr W. H. Cocker, the first mayor and freeman of the town. Alderman Walter Newman had the distinction of being the Mayor of Blackpool during the town's diamond jubilee year, which took place from 7 to 27 June 1936. Several events took place, including gymnastic displays, highland gatherings, beauty queen contests and a Royal Navy and military tournament accompanied by various military bands.

In August 2019, a stained-glass window that had been set into the ceiling in the Council Chamber was restored.

# Jean Robinson, First Female Mayor of Blackpool (1968–69)

Jean Robinson made history when she was elected Blackpool's first female mayor in 1968–69. Mayor Councillor Amy Cross, the youngest ever mayor when she was inaugurated into the role in May 2019, unveiled a blue plaque awarded by Blackpool Civic Trust, which holds pride of place in Abingdon Street Café where Jean worked for twenty-seven years. Deeply committed to Blackpool, where she served as councillor and mayor, it was a proud moment for her granddaughter and great-granddaughter, who commissioned the blue plaque on 11 January 2020. Jean blazed a trail for the election of female mayors in Blackpool and was followed by a total of thirteen ladies over the years following her election.

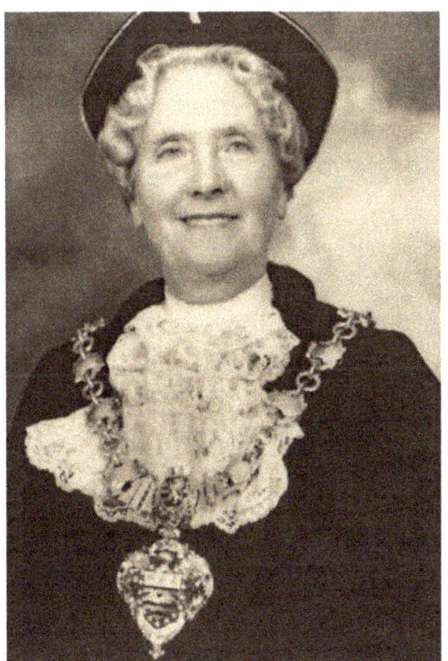

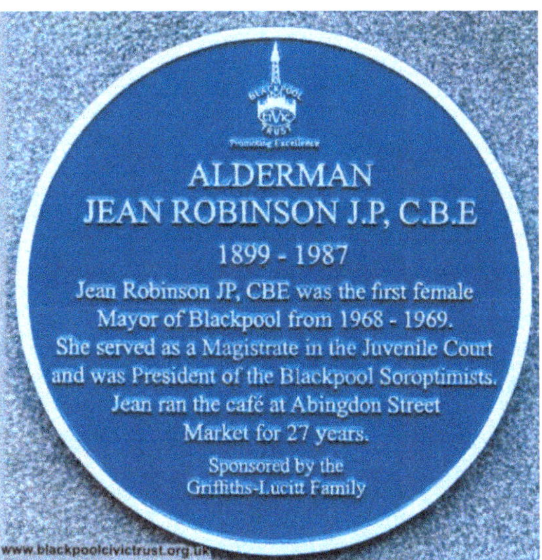


*Above left*: Jean Robinson – Blackpool's first female mayor.

*Above right*: Blue plaque commemorating Jean Robinson.

# 10

# Blackpool in Victory

In a prominent position on Blackpool Promenade, surrounded by three of Blackpool's most notable buildings – the Metropole Hotel, the North Pier, and the Town Hall on Talbot Road – are the resort's war memorial and cenotaph, erected in 1923. On the fourth anniversary of Great Britain's entry into the war, remembrance services were held in every city, town and village throughout the British Empire. The town's own remembrance service took place in the sunken gardens in front of the Hotel Metropole, where local people gathered to pay their respects. A temporary memorial was erected, consisting of two large, simple wooden crosses, and General T. E. Topping broadcast to the crowds via a loudspeaker placed at the top of a nearby tram shelter with a poignant message: 'Their names are engraved on stone, and even though, sad that is only in name, we have brought them home to their native town.'

After the war was over, the local community wanted to have a more permanent memorial to honour their dead. The first Remembrance Day was commemorated on 11 November 1919 and was known as Armistice Day, changing to Remembrance Day after the Second World War. However, it was not until 1923 that a 100-foot obelisk made of Cornish grey granite with large bronze relief

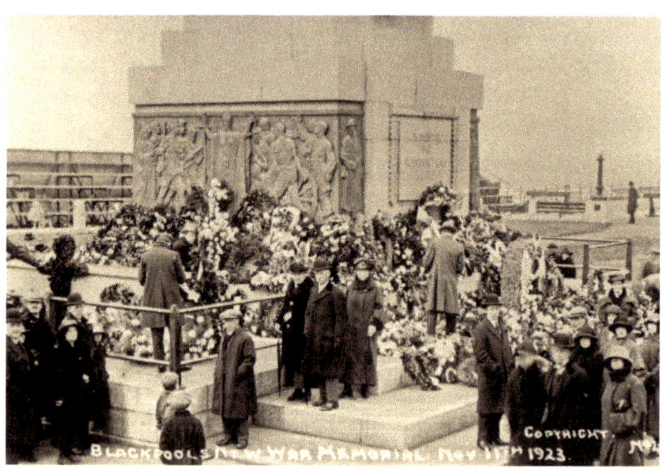


Blackpool War Memorial, 11 November 1923.

panels designed by Ernest Prestwich and sculpted by the renowned Gilbert Ledward, finally took pride of place where the temporary memorials had once stood. The sculptures are of a wife and child left behind after enlistment, a nurse, a grieving widow, a small girl and, an unusual choice, a German soldier.

At the end of the First World War, Blackpool, along with many other cities and towns, celebrated the country's victory. On 11 November 1918, a Peace Day celebration was held in Talbot Square, attended by thousands of people. Two bands attended and played the national anthem, 'Marseillaise', and 'Land of Hope and Glory'. A seaplane dropped thousands of leaflets announcing the signing of the Armistice, and the *Blackpool Gazette* reported, 'This is your VE Day.' Every street in the town was festooned with flags, and the Town Hall was decorated with flags of the Allied nations. Women wore red, white, and blue rosettes in their hair, while men and boys wore them in their buttonholes. Veterans of the last war and the Boer War proudly wore their medals as they joined in the celebrations. Arrangements were made for the prime minister's speech to be relayed to the crowds in Talbot Square through loudspeakers, and the mayor, Alderman John W. Roberts, addressed the crowd. A service was held in St John's Parish Church, which struggled to accommodate everyone who wished to attend. An American services band entertained the jubilant crowd as they waited for the arrival of the town's civic dignitaries.

In addition to the traditional Remembrance Day services in November every year, there have been other events such as the 'War Veterans Impressive March to the Cenotaph' (as it was reported in the press) that took place on 20 July 1930. To the inspiring music of the veteran's song '300 Mons Heroes', all members of the Old Contemptibles Association marched along the Promenade to lay a wreath at the cenotaph. They were inspected at the Central Pier by Colonel G. W. Gibson DSO of Lancaster, accompanied by the mayor (Councillor C. W. Gath), himself an ex-serviceman, and watched by 20,000 holidaymakers and residents.

In 1983, the cenotaph was awarded Grade II status, which in June 2017 was upgraded to Grade II* by Historic England. Major restoration work had been carried out in 2007/8 when the stonework and bronzes were cleaned and a new memorial to civilian casualties – *The Choir Loft* by artist Ruth Barker – was added. It was unveiled by the Duchess of Cornwall at a dedication service on 26 June 2008.

Since 2006, Blackpool Armed Forces Week has been celebrated every year, and in 2008 Blackpool beat four other cities to host the event. It officially begins with the raising of the armed forces flag above the Town Hall, followed by a week of special events (which have included themed tea dances in the Tower Ballroom), and on National Veterans Day members of the 12th Regiment Royal Artillery march along the Promenade past the Tower to the cenotaph. Crowds thrilled to the Battle of Britain memorial flight and the Red Devils parachute jump, followed by a spectacular firework display. On Saturday 29 June 2019 a special day of entertainment took place at Stanley Park, with displays of military vehicles in the Italian gardens. The day came to a rousing end with a live concert by the Band of

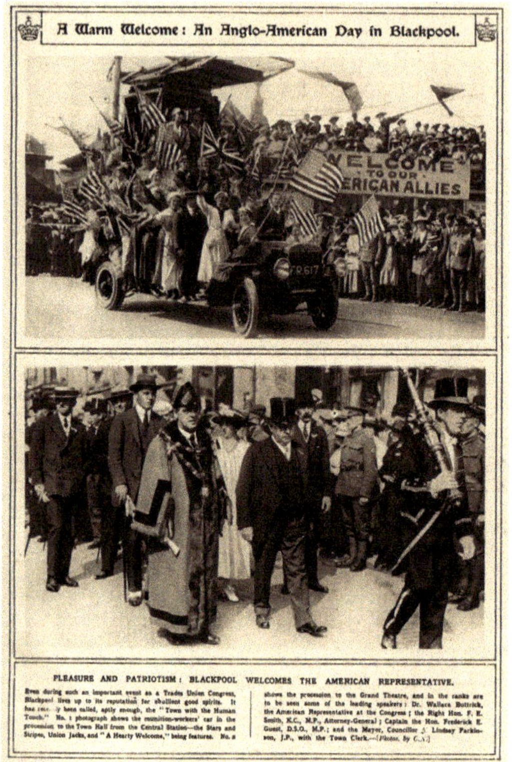


Anglo-American day at Blackpool.

Corps of Drums, Royal Regiment of Lancashire Fusiliers at the Norbreck Castle Hotel. On the Sunday morning, a service of appreciation and a parade took place at the war memorial, where crowds gathered just as they had on the inauguration ceremony ninety-six years earlier.

On the celebration of the 75th anniversary of Victory in Europe Day, Blackpool's key venues and attractions – including the Big Wheel on Central Pier, the dome on the Winter Gardens, the Promenade by the Hampton by Hilton Hotel, the seafront, cenotaph and Lightworks Illumination Depot – were illuminated in red, white, and blue over the bank holiday weekend. The heart of the Tower was transformed into a Union Flag, and the Town Hall bell rang out for five minutes at 3 p.m. This was also to celebrate the huge part that Blackpool and the Fylde Coast played in the wartime effort when thousands of servicemen and women were stationed in the resort, the airport being part of the air defence network, and nearby Warton the largest air base in Europe.

## Blackpool Continues to Celebrate

Following a long tradition of celebrating major events in the country, in June 2022 Blackpool unveiled a spectacular programme of entertainment to mark the

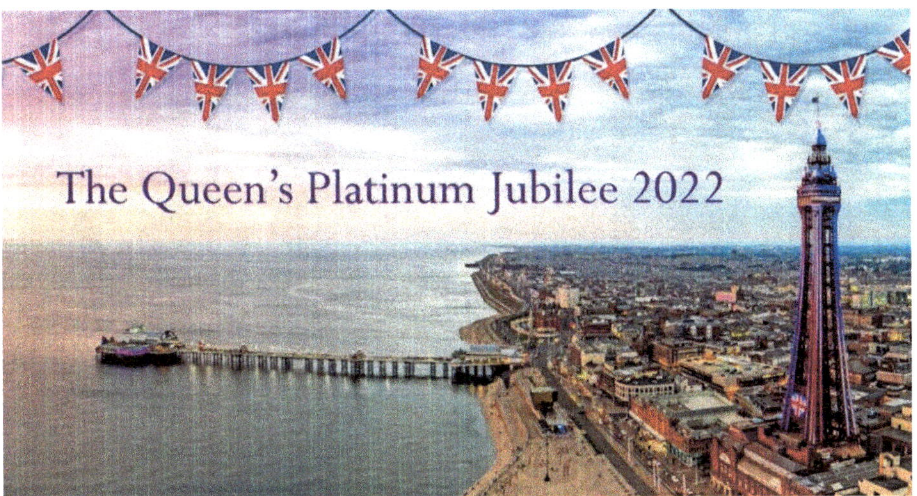


Queen's Platinum Jubilee, 2022.

Elizabeth II's platinum jubilee. A four-day public holiday, the event included a parade of heritage trams along the seafront, a light and laser show, and a burst of fireworks at the top of the Tower. About a dozen trams from the heritage fleet travelled in convoy from the Pleasure Beach to Little Bispham, forming one of the largest tram parades the resort has ever seen. The magnificent Tower took centre stage as it was lit up in red, white, and blue throughout the four days of celebration.

The town is one of thousands of locations across the UK where beacons were lit. Beacons were first introduced to mark the diamond jubilee of Queen Victoria and the 75th anniversary of VE Day, and were used to commemorate the occasion of Elizabeth II's ninetieth birthday in 2016.

## The Future of Blackpool

Taking Blackpool further into the twenty-first century, there are many exciting changes on the horizon. These include a £300 million entertainment complex to be built on the Golden Mile with a state-of-the-art Conference Centre between the Empress Ballroom and the Opera House. There will be new places to shop, eat and stay, like the new Premier Inn being constructed on Talbot Square, along with an extension to the tramway, and that is not all. An exciting new £13 million project to build a new museum in the Sands Hotel is being built on Central Promenade. The attraction is set to be the UK's first museum of circus, variety and magic, and is due to be open in the next couple of years.

These first-class attractions will attract even more visitors to the town and will ensure that Blackpool, whose byword has always been 'progress', will continue to be the entertainment capital of the UK, if not the world.

# Acknowledgements

The author would like to thank the following people and organisations for permission to use copyright material in this book. Writing a book during a pandemic when many buildings, such as the Central Library in Blackpool, are closed relies heavily on help from other available sources – not an easy task in such times.

A most valuable source is the picture postcard, which has depicted a huge array of themes of this popular seaside resort since the mid-1890s. I am also indebted to the following people and organisations for their help and permission to use their images, which have supplemented my own. My special thanks go to Ray Milburn, whose photographic skills have produced most of the modern photographs, and also to my niece, artist Judith Tanczos, for her drawing of Alderman Cocker. With thanks to the following: Robert Leach, David Slattery-Christy, John Burke, Kirk Atkinson, Elizabeth Gomm, Allan Wood and Chris Bottomley, Mary Evans Picture Library, Blackpool Heritage, Coronation Rock Co., and Blackpool Civic Trust.

Every attempt has been made to seek permission for copyright material used in this book. However, if we have inadvertently used copyright material without permission/acknowledgement we apologise and will make the necessary correction at the first opportunity.